Enola Prudhomme's
LOW-FAT
FAVORITES

Also by Enola Prudhomme:

Enola Prudhomme's Low-Calorie Cajun Cooking

Enola Prudhomme's LOW-FAT FAVORITES

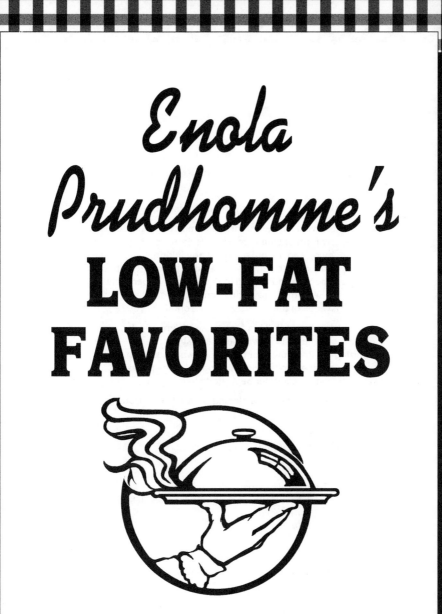

HEARST BOOKS

New York

It is the policy of William Morrow and Company, Inc.,
and its imprints and affiliates,
recognizing the importance of preserving what has been written,
to print the books we publish on acid-free paper,
and we exert our best efforts to that end.

Library of Congress Cataloging-in-Publication Data

Prudhomme, Enola.
    [Low-fat favorites]
    Enola Prudhomme's low-fat favorites — 1st ed.
        p.   cm
    Includes index.
    ISBN 0-688-11894-1 (alk. paper)
    1. Cookery, American—Southern style.   2. Low-fat diet—Recipes.
I.   Title.   II. Title: Low-fat favorites.
TX715.2.S68P78   1994
641.5'638—dc20   94-6973
                                                                      CIP

Printed in the United States of America

First Edition

1 2 3 4 5 6 7 8 9 10

BOOK DESIGN BY GIORGETTA BELL McREE

This cookbook is dedicated to the memory of the following mem-
bers of family:

To my sister Allie Fontenot. Allie used to tell me often how
proud she was to tell people I was her sister and Paul her brother,
for what we had accomplished. I would like to say I was equally
proud to have her for my sister.

To my sister-in-law K Hendrick Prudhomme. I worked for K and
Paul in New Orleans and saw K almost every day. Although she
kept a very hectic schedule, she always offered a cheerful smile
and a friendly hello.

To my special brother, Saul "Bobby" Prudhomme. Bobby
would often come to the cafe, and when he could, he loved to
come with us to caterings and festivals. . . . We miss you very
much.

To my sister-in-law Marie Prudhomme. Marie was a very special person. She was more like a mother to me . . . always there
to lend me a helping hand for many years.

Although they're no longer with us, they'll remain in my heart
forever.

Contents

Acknowledgments
ix

Introduction
xi

Notes from Our Kitchen
xiii

Soups
1

Salads and Salad Dressings
17

Shellfish
39

Fish
61

Chicken and Turkey
87

Beef, Pork and Other Meats
147

Vegetables
187

Casseroles and Stews
225

Pasta
245

Rice, Dressings
and Other Side Dishes
267

Dips, Salsas and Sauces
277

Breads, Muffins and Biscuits
291

Desserts
299

Index
317

Acknowledgments

Were it not for the talent, hard work and enthusiasm of the following people, this cookbook would not exist. I want to recognize them and offer my warmest thanks.

I deeply appreciate the efforts of Sandra Day, who worked as chief editor. Her kindness and patience are remarkable.

My daughter Diane Broussard has earned my respect and gratitude for organizing and writing this book. Her dedication to detail and her craftsmanship with the written word are superb.

My daughter Annette Oncale helped me test and retest countless recipes and kept my kitchen organized.

To Greg Sylvester, a custodian at our restaurant, I owe a special debt. I know at times it was difficult to have my skillets and testing equipment clean in a hurry, so thanks for coming through.

I am grateful to the entire staff at Prudhomme's Cajun Cafe for their support and eagerness to be my taste testers.

I am especially thankful to my husband, Shelton.

We owe a huge debt of gratitude to Ann Bramson, Harriet Bell and to all at William Morrow for their enthusiasm and support.

Introduction

I was born in Opelousas, Louisiana, and grew up with twelve brothers and sisters. We lived on a thriving farm in the bayou country, where food was plentiful. We all learned the art of hard work, and because there were so many of us, you can imagine the tremendous amount of food that had to be prepared. Mother was an excellent cook, and I learned how to cook from watching and helping her.

In 1985, I opened a restaurant in historical Washington, Louisiana. It was not very long, however, before the place seemed too small and I was looking for something larger. Call it fate if you will, but I found a beautiful old home built in the 1800s that seemed to beckon for the restaurant to take up residency and to make it come alive. So . . . I purchased it and moved.

It's been life in the fast lane ever since. With a thriving business, I keep a very hectic schedule. Besides co-authoring the *Prudhomme Family Cookbook,* I wrote *Enola Prudhomme's Low-Calorie Cajun Cooking* and have now completed my latest cookbook.

I was recently named 1993 Businesswoman of the Year by the Lafayette Economic and Development Association. Since my low-calorie Cajun cookbook was published in 1991, I have received hundreds of letters and phone calls from readers who tell me how much they enjoy my book, and how some have lost 20, 30 and up to 40 pounds. I would like to thank all the doctors and dieticians who have recommended my cookbook to patients with weight problems or other health concerns. It makes me feel good to know I've helped so many people. I hope anyone who uses this cookbook will enjoy it as much as I've enjoyed creating it. Call or write and let me know! Living life to its fullest is the only way to live!

C'est bon!
—ENOLA PRUDHOMME

Notes from Our Kitchen

Alligator
In South Louisiana, alligators are found in local swamps. We use only the tail section for cooking. The meat has a delicate flavor, somewhat like chicken white meat.

Bisque
A thick, rich Cajun soup, bisque is usually made with crawfish, shrimp or crabmeat.

Bread Crumbs
The bread crumbs used in this book are homemade from bread (40 calories per slice) that has been toasted and made into bread crumbs in the food processor or blender.

Broth
The broth used in this book is canned and salt-free. I use it often and I love the flavor. It is available in all supermarkets.

Browning and Seasoning Sauce
Made from caramelized sugar, this bottled dark-brown liquid is used to darken sauces and gravies.

Cornmeal
We are so serious about our cornmeal that we use only freshly ground yellow cornmeal, which is widely available in South Louisiana. Stone-ground cornmeal is available in supermarkets everywhere.

Cottage Cheese
Many of the recipes in this book call for low-fat cottage cheese blended until smooth before using.

Crabmeat
Fresh lump crabmeat is the only seafood I use that is precooked. It is readily available in supermarkets and seafood stores, usually in 1-pound plastic containers. Before using crabmeat in any recipe, be sure to pick through it to remove any stray pieces of shell or cartilage.

Crawfish
Crawfish are plentiful throughout Louisiana, and sometimes you can find them in your local markets, but if you can't find crawfish, substitute shrimp.

Creole Mustard
A specialty of Louisiana's German Creoles, this hot, spicy mustard is made from vinegar-marinated brown mustard seeds with a hint of horseradish. It is available in the gourmet section of most supermarkets.

Green Onions
Cajuns prefer the term *green onions* to *scallions,* and we use plenty of them in our cooking. We grow them year round in our backyards, so we always have plenty on hand.

Margarine
Only reduced-calorie margarine is used in my recipes because it is lower in fat and calories than butter.

Milk
Most of our recipes call for canned evaporated skim milk. A few recipes use regular skim milk, but never whole milk.

Mirliton
This gourdlike fruit is about the size and shape of a very large pear and is also known as the chayote or vegetable pear. In South Louisiana, however, it is better known as the mirliton. Look for small, firm, unblemished fruit.

Nonstick Vegetable Cooking Spray

I use cooking spray for oiling skillets, casseroles and such. Cooking spray contains fewer than 2½ calories per serving. In some recipes, I recommend using butter-flavored nonstick cooking spray.

Okra

Okra can be boiled, pickled or steamed. Okra varies in size from 1 to 8 inches in length, but the smaller the pod, the more tender it is. While nothing beats the taste of fresh okra, frozen okra will do.

Onions

I can't imagine cooking without onions. I use a combination of fresh and dehydrated onions in my recipes.

Oysters

If you are lucky enough to live near oyster beds that are harvested, use them. If you buy already shucked oysters in their liquor, don't throw the liquor away; use it to make seafood stock—it is too delicious to waste.

Peppers

Red and green bell peppers (fresh) are staples in my kitchen. For this new book I've added a few more varieties, such as Anaheim peppers, which are long, thin, pale-green chilies with a mild flavor; and serrano peppers, which are small, bright green, and very hot.

Quick-Mixing Flour

This unique flour makes lighter cuisine as simple as it is delicious. It is made by forming high-quality flour into "crystals" that mix instantly.

Rabbit
Use fresh domestic rabbit when possible. Dishes made with rabbit are growing in popularity because rabbit is low in calories and fat.

Rice
I use converted rice in all my recipes because it cooks faster and fluffier than regular rice.

Roux Flour
Traditionally, a roux, the basis of many Cajun dishes, is made from slowly heating oil and flour, but who needs all those extra calories? I've developed a roux that contains only flour—no oil! By simply browning the flour, you can achieve the same flavor as a traditional roux. Once made, roux flour will keep for several months if stored in a tightly covered container.

Salt-Free Chicken Bouillon Granules
You can find these in most supermarkets. Mix with water to use as stock in the recipes if homemade stock is not available.

Shrimp
While fresh-from-the-Gulf shrimp are always available in South Louisiana, any of these recipes can be prepared with shrimp found in your local market.

Stock
At the restaurant, we make our own homemade stock, whether chicken or seafood. Stock adds a rich, hearty flavor to almost any dish. It is simple to make, freezes well, and you can always double the recipe if you want to keep some on hand.

Turkey
Many of the recipes use turkey in place of beef or even chicken. Turkey is low in fat and calories and offers endless possibilities.

Tamales

The majority of the tamales—no matter what their filling, flavoring or wrapping—start with a dough of *masa para tamales* (corn dough for tamales) or *harina para tamales* (cornmeal for tamales), which are made from dried field corn that has been boiled briefly with slaked lime, hulled and coarsely ground. If the treated corn is dried before grinding, it makes meal; if ground wet, it becomes a coarse-textured dough.

Vegetables

Whenever possible, use fresh vegetables that are in season. There are times you may have to use frozen vegetables, but when properly prepared, frozen okra, corn, peas and spinach can be just as delicious as fresh. Many of the vegetable recipes reflect the Cajun way of cooking vegetables—long, slow cooking. If you prefer your vegetables less well done, adjust the cooking times accordingly.

SOUPS

Chicken Stock

MAKES ABOUT 4 QUARTS

*5½ pounds meaty chicken
  bones or chicken wings
  and backs*
*2 medium onions, unpeeled
  and quartered*
8 quarts water
*2 medium carrots, cut in
  half lengthwise*

*1 bunch green onions
  (white part only)*
1 bunch fresh parsley stems
10 black peppercorns
2 bay leaves

Preheat the oven to 400°F.

Place the chicken bones or wings and backs and the onions in a 5-quart Dutch oven. Bake for 45 minutes, or until browned. Remove the pot from the oven and add *half* of the water, stirring and scraping the bottom of the pot until all the brown bits are loosened.

Transfer everything to a large stockpot and place over high heat. Add the remaining quarts of water and all the rest of the ingredients and bring to a boil.

Reduce the heat to medium and simmer, uncovered, for 20 minutes. Cover, reduce the heat and simmer for 2 to 3 hours, or until the liquid has been reduced by half. Remove the stock from the heat and strain through a sieve, discarding all the remains. Allow the stock to cool slightly, then refrigerate overnight.

The next day, using a spoon, skim all the congealed fat from the top of the stock before using. Refrigerate or freeze the stock in covered containers until needed.

NUTRITIONAL INFORMATION NOT AVAILABLE.

Dessire's Lemon-Chicken Soup

After my great-granddaughter Dessire polished off a big bowl of this lemon-scented chicken soup, she turned to her Mom and asked, "Would you make some of this for me tomorrow?"

MAKES 4½ CUPS

5 cups Chicken Stock
(page 3)
½ cup quick-cooking rice
2 tablespoons lemon juice

1 tablespoon finely chopped
fresh parsley
1 teaspoon salt
¼ teaspoon ground white
pepper

In a large stockpot over high heat, bring the chicken stock to a boil. Add the rice; reduce the heat to a simmer and cook, covered, for 15 minutes, or until the rice is tender. Add the remaining ingredients and cook 2 minutes longer. Serve hot.

PER CUP	KCAL	FATgm	CHOLmg	SODmg
	88	0.1	0	500

Chicken-Vegetable Soup

This delicious soup can be frozen for up to 2 months in a tightly covered container. You'll want to keep some handy for busy days. All you will have to do is heat and serve!

MAKES 10 CUPS

12 cups water
One 2½-pound chicken, skinned and quartered
One 16-ounce can salt-free whole tomatoes
2 medium carrots, thinly sliced
1 cup chopped onions
1 cup chopped celery

1 cup peeled and cubed potatoes
1 cup sweet peas
1 cup whole-kernel corn
2 teaspoons salt
1 teaspoon dried basil leaves, crushed
1 teaspoon ground red pepper

In an 8-quart stockpot over high heat, bring the water to a boil. Add the chicken and cook for 10 minutes. Reduce the heat to medium. Add all the remaining ingredients and cook, covered, for 45 minutes, or until the chicken is tender. Remove the chicken and let cool to the touch. Debone the chicken, then cut into bite-size pieces. Return the chicken to the pot and cook 15 minutes longer, stirring occasionally.

PER CUP	KCAL	FATgm	CHOLmg	SODmg
	218	5.9	77	502

Chicken-Tomato Soup with Pasta

*A*ny *pasta will work well in this soup. I use angelhair pasta because it has such a delicate look. If there are any leftovers, you can freeze them in a tightly covered container until ready to use.*

MAKES 8 CUPS

8 cups water
1 pound skinned and boned
    chicken breasts, cut
    into 1-inch strips
1 medium potato, peeled
    and cut into 2-inch
    cubes
1 medium carrot, sliced
    (about 1 cup)

1 cup chopped onions
One 16-ounce can salt-free
    whole tomatoes
2 ounces angelhair pasta
1½ teaspoons salt
½ teaspoon dried basil
    leaves, crushed

In a 6-quart Dutch oven over medium heat, bring the water to a boil. Add the chicken, potato, carrot, onions and tomatoes; cover, reduce the heat and cook for 35 minutes, stirring occasionally. Add the pasta, salt and basil and cook, uncovered, 10 minutes longer, stirring often.

PER CUP	KCAL	FATgm	CHOLmg	SODmg
	143	2.3	48	421

6

Spicy Beef Orzo Soup

A hearty beef-vegetable soup with orzo, a rice-shaped pasta. Use less pepper if you prefer less spice.

MAKES 10 CUPS

12 cups water
1 pound boneless beef
    round steak, cut into
    bite-size pieces
One 16-ounce can salt-free
    whole tomatoes, cut
    into bite-size pieces

1 cup finely chopped onions
2 cups chopped fresh green
    beans
1/2 cup orzo
1 teaspoon salt
1 teaspoon ground white
    pepper

In a 5-quart Dutch oven over high heat, bring the water to a boil. Add the meat, tomatoes and onions and cook for 30 minutes, stirring often. Add the green beans, orzo, salt and pepper; continue cooking for 20 minutes, or until the meat is tender. Serve hot.

PER CUP	KCAL	FATgm	CHOLmg	SODmg
	243	8.3	68	359

Simple Vegetable Soup

*C*hances are good that you have everything you need to make this soup on hand. *Keep individual portions in the freezer (up to 3 months), and instead of reaching for those cookies or chips, pop some soup in the microwave and enjoy.*

MAKES 14 CUPS

10 cups water
2 tablespoons salt-free beef
*   bouillon granules*
Two 14-ounce cans stewed
*   tomatoes*
One 16-ounce can French-
*   style green beans*
One 10-ounce package
*   frozen mixed vegetables*
One 10-ounce package
*   frozen whole kernel*
*   corn*

1 cup chopped onions
½ cup chopped celery
½ cup chopped green bell
*   pepper*
½ cup chopped red bell
*   pepper*
1 teaspoon salt
¼ teaspoon ground white
*   pepper*
½ cup orzo

In a 5-quart Dutch oven over high heat, bring the water to a boil. Add the beef bouillon granules, stirring well. Add all the remaining ingredients *except* the orzo; cook, covered, for 30 minutes. Reduce the heat to a simmer, add the orzo and cook 20 minutes longer, stirring occasionally.

PER CUP	KCAL	FATgm	CHOLmg	SODmg
	81	0.8	1	387

Shrimp Chowder

A *hearty chowder with the delicate flavor of shrimp.*

MAKES 10 CUPS

1 tablespoon reduced-
    calorie margarine
3 cups peeled and cubed
    potatoes
¼ pound Canadian bacon,
    cut into ½-inch cubes
1 cup chopped onions
½ teaspoon salt
½ teaspoon ground white
    pepper

2 tablespoons salt-free beef
    bouillon granules
2 cups water
2 cups evaporated skim
    milk
24 large shrimp, peeled and
    deveined
½ cup finely chopped green
    onions

Melt the margarine in a 5-quart Dutch oven over high heat. Add *2 cups* of the potatoes, the bacon, onions, salt and white pepper. Cook for 15 minutes, stirring often. Dissolve the bouillon granules in water and add to the pot along with the milk and remaining potatoes. Cover and cook for 20 minutes, or until the potatoes are tender, stirring often. Transfer *half* of the potato mixture to a food processor and process until smooth; return to the pot. Add the shrimp and green onions; cook, covered, 10 minutes longer.

PER CUP	KCAL	FATgm	CHOLmg	SODmg
	139	3	101	540

Crabmeat Bisque

If fresh lump crabmeat is not available, you can substitute three 6-ounce cans fancy white crabmeat for this dish.

MAKES 5 CUPS

7 cups water
½ cup Roux Flour
  (page 289)
5 tablespoons tomato paste
1 cup very finely chopped
  onions
¼ cup very finely chopped
  celery
¼ cup very finely chopped
  bell pepper
1 teaspoon salt

⅛ teaspoon ground white
  pepper
¼ teaspoon ground red
  pepper
1 pound fresh lump
  crabmeat, picked over
¼ cup very finely chopped
  green onions
2 tablespoons very finely
  chopped fresh parsley

In a 5-quart Dutch oven over high heat, bring *6 cups* of the water to a boil. Add the roux flour and stir until dissolved. Stir the tomato paste into the remaining 1 cup water and add to the pot along with the onions, celery, bell pepper, salt and peppers. Cook for 35 minutes, stirring occasionally. Add the crabmeat, green onions and parsley. Cover and cook 10 minutes longer.

PER CUP	KCAL	FATgm	CHOLmg	SODmg
	140	1	37	1373

Eggplant Soup

We use lots of eggplant at our restaurant, so there's always some extra for this soup. Freeze any leftovers.

MAKES 8 CUPS

1 pound skinned and boned
  chicken breasts, cut
  into ½-inch strips
2 teaspoons salt
¼ teaspoon ground white
  pepper
¼ teaspoon celery seed
2 tablespoons reduced-
  calorie margarine
1 pound peeled and
  chopped eggplant

1 small onion, quartered
1 medium tomato, peeled,
  seeded and chopped
4 cups water
1 tablespoon finely chopped
  red bell pepper
1 tablespoon finely chopped
  green onion

Spray the inside of a medium skillet with nonstick vegetable cooking spray and place over high heat. Add the chicken and sprinkle with the salt, white pepper and celery seed. Cook for 10 minutes, or until the chicken is browned; remove from the heat and set aside.

Melt the margarine in a 5-quart Dutch oven over high heat. Add the eggplant, onion and tomato; cook and stir for 10 minutes. Stir in *1 cup* of the water and cook 5 minutes longer. Pour the mixture into the container of a food processor and process till smooth, then return to the Dutch oven along with the chicken, remaining 3 cups water, bell pepper and green onion; cook, covered, 15 minutes longer.

PER CUP	KCAL	FATgm	CHOLmg	SODmg
	124	3.6	48	205

Cabbage and Leek Soup

The leek is a member of the onion family; it resembles a giant green onion with overlapping wide, green leaves, a fat white stalk, and shaggy roots at the bulb end. Avoid leeks that are larger than 1½ inches in diameter because they'll be less tender. Clean the leeks thoroughly to remove sand and dirt.

MAKES 4 CUPS

1 tablespoon reduced-calorie margarine
2 large potatoes, peeled and cut into 1-inch cubes
2 cups shredded cabbage
1 large leek, thinly sliced
2 cloves garlic, minced
½ teaspoon salt
½ teaspoon ground white pepper

3 tablespoons salt-free chicken bouillon granules
4 cups water
¼ cup very finely chopped green onions
1 tablespoon very finely chopped fresh parsley

Melt the margarine in a 5-quart Dutch oven over high heat. Add the next 6 ingredients and sauté for 10 minutes. Dissolve the bouillon granules in the water and add to the pot. Cover and cook for 30 minutes, stirring often. Remove from the heat. Using a slotted spoon, spoon *half* of the vegetables into a food processor and process until smooth. Return to the pot and place over medium heat. Cook, stirring, 2 minutes longer. Garnish with the chopped green onion and parsley.

PER SERVING	KCAL	FATgm	CHOLmg	SODmg
	145	3.9	5	438

Cauliflower Soup

*C*auliflower becomes light and mild when turned into soup.

MAKES 6 CUPS

4 cups Chicken Stock
    (page 3)
1 cup finely chopped onions
3 cups fresh
    cauliflowerettes
1 medium carrot, thinly
    sliced

1 cup skim milk
1 cup evaporated skim milk
1 teaspoon salt
¼ teaspoon ground white
    pepper
⅛ teaspoon ground nutmeg

In a large stockpot over medium heat, cook the stock and onions for 10 minutes, stirring occasionally. Add the cauliflower and carrot and cook for 20 minutes, or until the vegetables are tender. Using a slotted spoon, transfer the carrots and cauliflower to a small bowl; mash them with a fork, then return to the pot. Add the milk, salt, white pepper and nutmeg; continue cooking for 25 minutes, stirring often.

PER ½ CUP	KCAL	FATgm	CHOLmg	SODmg
	66	0.6	3	349

Tex-Mex Lentil Soup

Chockablock with vegetables and border spices—perfect for those cold winter nights.

MAKES 12 CUPS

½ pound dried lentils
2 tablespoons olive oil
1 cup chopped onions
1 cup chopped celery
½ cup finely chopped red
  bell pepper
8 cups Chicken Stock
  (page 3)
Two 16-ounce cans whole-
  kernel corn
2 large tomatoes, peeled,
  seeded and chopped
2 small turnips, peeled and
  diced
2 bay leaves
2 cups dried lima beans

1 cup chopped green chili
  peppers
1 tablespoon ground cumin
1 tablespoon ground
  coriander
1½ teaspoons salt
½ teaspoon ground white
  pepper
½ teaspoon ground red
  pepper
½ teaspoon ground black
  pepper
¼ cup very finely chopped
  fresh parsley
3 tablespoons lemon juice

Rinse the lentils and soak in cold water for 2 hours, then drain and set aside. In a 5-quart Dutch oven over high heat, heat the oil. Add the onions, celery and bell pepper and sauté for 5 minutes. Add the lentils and all the remaining ingredients *except* the parsley and lemon juice. Bring to a boil.

Reduce the heat to medium. Cook for 30 minutes, stirring often. Add the parsley and lemon juice and cook 10 minutes longer. Remove the bay leaves before serving.

PER CUP	KCAL	FATgm	CHOLmg	SODmg
	117	3.8	2	205

Cajun Gazpacho

*H*ere *in Cajun country, cold soup is rarely served, but this one is great on a hot summer day.*

MAKES 5 CUPS

*1 roasted yellow bell pepper
   (page 220), chopped
6 medium tomatoes, peeled,
   seeded and chopped
One 16-ounce can salt-free
   tomato juice
2 cups chopped iceberg
   lettuce*

*½ cup chopped green
   onions
2 tablespoons balsamic
   vinegar
¼ teaspoon salt
⅛ teaspoon ground red
   pepper
1½ cups ice water*

Place all the ingredients *except* the water in a large bowl and mix well. Put *half* of the mixture in a blender and process until smooth. Pour into the bowl with the remaining mixture and mix well. Stir in the water and chill before serving.

PER CUP	KCAL	FATgm	CHOLmg	SODmg
	40	0.4	0	118

SALADS
AND SALAD
DRESSINGS

Sweet Pea Salad

For as long as I can remember, my family has enjoyed sweet pea salad at every holiday celebration and special occasion. This is my low-fat version of a Southern favorite.

MAKES 4 SERVINGS

One 16-ounce can sweet
  peas, drained
⅓ cup finely chopped red
  bell pepper
¼ cup finely chopped sweet
  pickles
3 tablespoons finely
  chopped pimiento-
  stuffed olives

1 tablespoon very finely
  chopped celery
1 hard-cooked egg, peeled
  and chopped
⅓ cup plain low-fat yogurt
1 tablespoon reduced-
  calorie mayonnaise
1 teaspoon balsamic
  vinegar

Combine all the ingredients in a medium bowl. Stir until well mixed and refrigerate for 1 hour before serving.

PER SERVING	KCAL	FATgm	CHOLmg	SODmg
	93	3.2	71	218

Three-Bean Salad

T ry this salad with Tomato Vinaigrette (page 36) instead of the vinegar, lemon juice, and oil listed in the ingredients.

MAKES EIGHT ⅔-CUP SERVINGS

One 17-ounce can lima
beans
One 15-ounce can red
kidney beans
One 15-ounce can garbanzo
beans
1 medium tomato, peeled,
seeded and chopped
½ cup very finely chopped
green bell pepper
⅓ cup very finely chopped
red bell pepper

⅓ cup chopped dill pickle
3 tablespoons balsamic
vinegar
3 tablespoons lemon juice
1 tablespoon olive oil
1 teaspoon granulated
garlic
1 teaspoon ground black
pepper

Drain all the liquid from the beans and rinse well. In a large bowl, combine the beans and all the remaining ingredients, stirring to mix well. Refrigerate until ready to serve.

PER SERVING	KCAL	FATgm	CHOLmg	SODmg
	230	6.5	0	777

Carrot and Raisin Salad

*S*outherners *like dishes that combine sweet and salty flavors. This classic is simple to prepare and can be served with anything.*

*2 cups shredded carrots
1 cup raisins
¼ cup skim milk*

*1 tablespoon reduced-
    calorie mayonnaise
2 packets sugar substitute*

Combine all the ingredients in a large bowl and mix well. Refrigerate for 1 hour before serving.

PER CUP	KCAL	FATgm	CHOLmg	SODmg
	97	2.3	4	79

Taco Salad

While judging a cooking contest in Houston, Texas, I had lunch at a small cafe where I was served a dish similar to this. It's dynamite!

MAKES 2 SERVINGS

FOR THE SALSA
2 large tomatoes, peeled and finely chopped
1 fresh jalapeño pepper, very finely chopped
1 clove garlic, minced
2 tablespoons very finely chopped onion
2 tablespoons very finely chopped green bell pepper
2 tablespoons very finely chopped celery
2 teaspoons olive oil

FOR THE FILLING
1 teaspoon chili powder
¼ teaspoon salt
¼ teaspoon granulated garlic
¼ teaspoon ground red pepper
½ pound beef flank steak, cut into ½-inch strips

FOR THE SALAD
8 large lettuce leaves
2 cups torn iceberg lettuce
2 small tomatoes, peeled and finely chopped

Combine all the salsa ingredients in a medium bowl and mix well. Cover and refrigerate for 1 hour, or until chilled.

Combine all dry seasonings for the filling in a small bowl. Mix well and sprinkle over the meat. Cover and refrigerate at least 4 hours to marinate. Spray the inside of a heavy iron skillet with nonstick vegetable cooking spray and place over high heat.

When very hot, add the meat and sauté for 10 minutes, or until browned. Remove from the heat and keep warm.

On each of 2 salad plates, arrange 4 lettuce leaves. Toss together the torn lettuce and tomatoes; mound on individual leaves, then top with the meat. Pour the salsa into 2 individual small bowls to serve on the side.

PER SERVING	KCAL	FATgm	CHOLmg	SODmg
	353	14.8	92	435

Potato Salad

A *low-fat version of a traditional favorite, it goes well with baked chicken.*

MAKES 6 SERVINGS

3 cups water
1 pound potatoes, peeled and cut into ½-inch cubes
¼ pound Canadian bacon, diced
½ roasted green bell pepper (page 220), diced
½ roasted red bell pepper, diced
¼ teaspoon salt
2 tablespoons minced onion

2 tablespoons fat-free sour cream
2 tablespoons reduced-calorie mayonnaise
1 tablespoon Dijon mustard
½ teaspoon ground black pepper

In a large saucepan over high heat, bring the water to a boil. Add the potatoes and cook for 10 minutes then drain. Place the potatoes in a medium bowl and set aside. Spray the inside of a small skillet with nonstick vegetable cooking spray and place over high heat. Add the bacon and sauté for 1 minute. Remove from the heat and add to the boiled potatoes along with the roasted peppers and salt; stir well.

In a small bowl, combine the remaining ingredients. Mix well and add to the potatoes, stirring well. Serve warm or cold.

PER SERVING	KCAL	FATgm	CHOLmg	SODmg
	113	2.9	11	363

Cabbage Slaw

After perfecting this dish, I tripled the ingredients, and our chef Chris served it as a side dish for lunch. Our customers loved it and asked that we put it on the menu.

MAKES 6 CUPS

4 cups shredded cabbage
¼ red bell pepper, thinly sliced
¼ cup finely chopped green onions, including tops
2 ribs celery, thinly sliced
¼ cup reduced-calorie mayonnaise

¼ cup fat-free sour cream
3 tablespoons white wine
2 tablespoons apple cider
1 teaspoon cracked black pepper
½ teaspoon granulated garlic
¼ teaspoon salt

Place the cabbage, bell pepper, green onions and celery in a large bowl; set aside. In a small bowl, combine all the remaining ingredients, stirring well. Pour over the cabbage mixture, mix well and serve.

PER CUP SERVING	KCAL	FATgm	CHOLmg	SODmg
	48	1.8	4	139

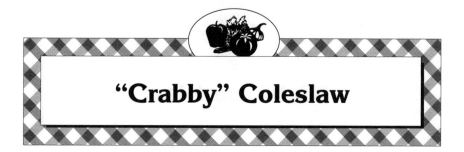

"Crabby" Coleslaw

Substituting two 6-ounce cans of tuna for the crabmeat works well in this recipe and makes a very affordable meal.

MAKES 3 SERVINGS

*½ cup reduced-calorie
   mayonnaise*
*¼ cup very finely chopped
   onion*
*¼ cup very finely chopped
   green bell pepper*
*¼ cup very finely chopped
   red bell pepper*
2 tablespoons wine vinegar
*2 tablespoons Dijon
   mustard*

½ teaspoon garlic powder
¼ teaspoon salt
¼ teaspoon dried dillweed
4 cups shredded cabbage
*12 ounces fresh lump
   crabmeat, picked over*
3 large lettuce leaves
6 cherry tomatoes

Combine the first 9 ingredients in a large bowl and mix well. Add the cabbage and mix well. Add the crabmeat and toss. Place each lettuce leaf on a 6-inch plate. Spoon 1 cup of the cabbage mixture on each leaf and garnish with 2 cherry tomatoes.

PER SERVING	KCAL	FATgm	CHOLmg	SODmg
	207	12	18	231

Broccoli and Cabbage Slaw

*D*on't throw away those broccoli stems—they're good for you. Be sure to cut and discard about 1 inch from the bottom of each stem. (The very bottom has a tendency to be tough.) Using a sharp paring knife, carefully peel the stems upward, using only the tender parts.

MAKES 6 CUPS

4 broccoli stems
3 cups shredded cabbage
1 large carrot, shredded
¼ cup reduced-calorie
    mayonnaise
¼ cup fat-free sour cream

3 tablespoons honey
1 tablespoon Dijon mustard
1 teaspoon celery seed
½ teaspoon ground black
    pepper
¼ teaspoon salt

Place the broccoli stems, one at a time, in a food processor and process until finely chopped. Transfer to a large bowl, add the cabbage and carrot and set aside. In a small bowl, combine all the remaining ingredients, stirring well. Pour over the broccoli, cabbage and carrot and mix well. Serve at room temperature or chill before serving if desired.

PER CUP SERVING	KCAL	FATgm	CHOLmg	SODmg
	87	2	4	147

Sweet Potato Slaw with Raisin Dressing

I *served this dish to Sheriff and Mrs. Don Breaux on one of their visits to the restaurant. The sheriff had recently undergone an angioplasty for his heart. He had to learn to eat healthy and his doctor had told him about my cookbook. Both he and Mrs. Breaux were surprised at how great the food tasted without all the fat.*

MAKES 5 CUPS

1 large sweet potato, peeled and grated (about 2 cups)
1 unpeeled red apple, diced
2 tablespoons lemon juice
3 cups shredded cabbage
1 cup evaporated skim milk
1 cup raisins

1 tablespoon sugar or 2 packets sugar substitute
1/4 teaspoon salt
3 tablespoons all-purpose flour
2 tablespoons water
2 tablespoons apple cider
1/8 teaspoon ground nutmeg

Bring a small saucepan of water to a boil over high heat. Add the sweet potato and cook for a few seconds, or until blanched. Remove from the heat and drain, then place in ice cold water, stirring to cool. Drain again, pressing with a spoon to remove any excess water. Pat the sweet potato dry with paper towels and separate with a fork; place in a large bowl.

Mix the apple with the lemon juice (this prevents the apple from turning brown), then add to the sweet potato along with the cabbage; toss and set aside.

In a medium skillet over high heat, bring the milk to a boil. Reduce the heat to low and add the raisins, sugar and salt. Cook and stir for 2 minutes. Dissolve the flour in the water and add to the skillet. Using a wire whisk, constantly whisk and continue cooking until the sauce starts to thicken. Remove from the heat and continue whisking until the sauce cools. Stir in the cider and nutmeg. Pour over the sweet potato mixture, mixing well.

Note: Be careful not to overcook the sweet potato or it will be too mushy. Have your ice water handy so you can start the cooling process. Also, if you choose to use the artificial sweetener, add it with the nutmeg.

PER CUP SERVING	KCAL	FATgm	CHOLmg	SODmg
	226	<1	2	176

Buttermilk Salad Dressing

*T*his is great as a salad dressing. I use this mixture in many of my recipes, so keep some handy.

MAKES 1½ CUPS

1 cup buttermilk
2 teaspoons vegetable oil
2 teaspoons dehydrated
    onion

2 teaspoons granulated
    garlic
½ teaspoon sugar
½ teaspoon salt

Combine all ingredients in a small glass bowl and mix well. Store in a tightly covered container and refrigerate till ready to use.

PER TABLESPOON	KCAL	FATgm	CHOLmg	SODmg
	8.60	.47	.38	51.53

Creamy Dill Dressing

Use this dressing as a topping for grilled or broiled fish.

MAKES 2 CUPS

*1 cup reduced-calorie
    mayonnaise
½ cup buttermilk
2 tablespoons evaporated
    skim milk
2 tablespoons finely
    chopped green onion*

*2 tablespoons minced dill
    pickle
1½ teaspoons celery seed
1 tablespoon Dijon mustard
1 teaspoon sugar*

Place all the ingredients in a blender and process until smooth. Store in a tightly covered container and refrigerate until ready to use.

PER TABLESPOON	KCAL	FATgm	CHOLmg	SODmg
	24	2	3	15

Lemon-Parmesan Dressing

Y*ou'll want to keep this dressing handy. It's great on salads, but try it on all kinds of pasta for an extra treat!*

MAKES 1 CUP

*½ cup reduced-calorie
    mayonnaise
¼ cup buttermilk
¼ cup freshly grated
    Parmesan cheese
2 tablespoons lemon juice*

*1 tablespoon olive oil
1 tablespoon low-sodium
    Worcestershire sauce
½ teaspoon minced fresh
    garlic*

Combine all the ingredients in a blender and process until smooth. Store in a tightly covered container in the refrigerator until ready to serve.

PER TABLESPOON	KCAL	FATgm	CHOLmg	SODmg
	38	3.4	4	37

Thousand Island Dressing

Bottled Thousand Island dressing is extra high in fat. Our customers rave about this homemade low-fat version.

MAKES 1 CUP

1 hard-cooked egg, peeled and finely chopped
½ cup reduced-calorie mayonnaise
¼ cup bottled chili sauce
2 tablespoons very finely chopped dill pickle

2 tablespoons very finely chopped green onion
2 teaspoons very finely chopped fresh parsley
1 teaspoon low-sodium Worcestershire sauce

In a medium bowl, combine all the ingredients and mix well. Store in a tightly covered container and refrigerate until ready to use.

PER TABLESPOON	KCAL	FATgm	CHOLmg	SODmg
	27	2.4	20	14

Tomato and Cucumber Dressing

*U*se this dressing on green salads, or pour it over slices of garden-fresh tomato and cucumbers.

MAKES 1 CUP

One 6-ounce can tomato
   juice
1 small cucumber, peeled,
   seeded and chopped
   (about ½ cup)
¼ cup chopped green
   onions
¼ cup chopped fresh
   parsley

2 tablespoons drained
   chopped pimiento
2 tablespoons lemon juice
1 tablespoon minced fresh
   garlic
1 teaspoon low-sodium
   Worcestershire sauce

Place all the ingredients in a blender and process until smooth. Store in a tightly covered container in the refrigerator until ready to use.

PER TABLESPOON	KCAL	FATgm	CHOLmg	SODmg
	5	0	0	40

Sour Cream Dressing

MAKES 1½ CUPS

½ cup fat-free sour cream
½ cup fat-free mayonnaise
¼ cup evaporated skim
    milk
2 tablespoons minced red
    onion

1 tablespoon minced red
    bell pepper
1 tablespoon Dijon mustard
1 teaspoon hot pepper
    sauce

Combine all the ingredients in a medium bowl and mix well. Refrigerate until ready to use.

PER TABLESPOON	KCAL	FATgm	CHOLmg	SODmg
	5	0	0	15

Tomato Vinaigrette

This vinaigrette gives any boring green salad a kick start.

MAKES 1 CUP

*2 plum tomatoes, peeled,
  seeded and chopped
  (about 1 cup)*
¼ cup white wine vinegar
1 tablespoon olive oil
2 cloves garlic, minced

1 packet sugar substitute
¼ teaspoon salt
¼ teaspoon dried oregano
*1 tablespoon minced fresh
  parsley*

Place all the ingredients *except* the parsley in a blender and process until smooth. Stir in the parsley. Store in a tightly covered container and refrigerate until ready to use.

PER TABLESPOON	KCAL	FATgm	CHOLmg	SODmg
	11	0.9	0	32

Cranberry Vinaigrette

*P*erfect for your holiday salads.

Makes 2 cups

One 8-ounce can cranberry
    sauce
One 6-ounce can cranberry
    juice
⅓ cup balsamic vinegar
¼ cup very finely chopped
    red onion

3 tablespoons prepared
    yellow mustard
3 tablespoons prepared
    brown mustard
1 teaspoon hot pepper
    sauce

Combine all the ingredients in a medium bowl. Beat with a wire whisk until smooth.

PER TABLESPOON	KCAL	FATgm	CHOLmg	SODmg
	15	0.1	0	22

SHELLFISH

Crab-Stuffed Party Tomatoes

This is a wonderful appetizer to serve for any gathering. It's sure to be a crowd pleaser!

MAKES 4 SERVINGS

1 pound cherry tomatoes
½ cup very finely chopped onions
½ cup very finely chopped bell pepper
½ cup water
2 tablespoons lemon juice
1 tablespoon low-sodium Worcestershire sauce
¼ teaspoon salt
¼ teaspoon ground white pepper
¼ teaspoon ground red pepper
2 slices bread (40 calories per slice), toasted and finely crumbled
One 6-ounce can fancy white crabmeat
2 tablespoons reduced-calorie mayonnaise

Wash the tomatoes and remove their stems. Slice ¼ inch from the top of each, reserving the tops. Scoop out the seeds from each tomato, then place upside down and set aside. Spray the inside of a medium skillet with butter-flavored nonstick vegetable cooking spray. Add the onions and bell pepper and sauté for 5 minutes, stirring constantly to prevent burning. Add the water; cook and stir 5 minutes more.

Add all the remaining ingredients; remove from the heat and mix well. Spoon equal amounts of the crabmeat mixture into each tomato. Place a reserved top on each tomato and serve.

PER SERVING	KCAL	FATgm	CHOLmg	SODmg
	113	3.3	45	421

Tangy Sautéed Shrimp with Pepper-Lime Sauce

½ teaspoon salt
½ teaspoon ground white
   pepper
½ teaspoon chili powder
1 pound medium shrimp,
   peeled and deveined
1 tablespoon reduced-
   calorie margarine
1 medium onion, thinly
   sliced
1 yellow bell pepper,
   roasted and thinly
   sliced

1 red bell pepper, roasted
   and thinly sliced
1 medium poblano pepper,
   roasted and thinly
   sliced
½ cup white wine
2 tablespoons balsamic
   vinegar
1 dried hot chili pepper,
   crushed
3 tablespoons lime juice
1 tablespoon finely chopped
   fresh parsley

Sprinkle the salt, white pepper and chili powder over the shrimp; set aside. Melt the margarine in a medium skillet over medium heat. Add the onion and sauté for 2 minutes. Add the roasted peppers and shrimp; cook, stirring, for 10 minutes. Add the wine and vinegar; cook and stir for 5 minutes. Remove from the heat. Spoon *half* of the onion and peppers into a food processor with dried chili and lime juice and process until smooth. Return to the same skillet and place over high heat; bring to a boil. Remove from the heat and stir in the parsley.

PER SERVING	KCAL	FATgm	CHOLmg	SODmg
	125	1.9	148	382

Lemon-Pepper Horseradish Shrimp

The lemon-pepper seasoning gives the shrimp a delicious tangy flavor.

MAKES 4 SERVINGS

1 cup water
½ pound medium shrimp, peeled and deveined
1 teaspoon salt
1 cup fat-free mayonnaise
¼ cup liquid from canned baby corn
¼ cup reserved shrimp stock
3 tablespoons very finely chopped onion
2 tablespoons very finely chopped green onion

2 tablespoons salt-free lemon-pepper seasoning
1 tablespoon low-sodium Worcestershire sauce
1 tablespoon lemon juice
1 teaspoon granulated garlic
½ teaspoon Dijon mustard
½ teaspoon hot pepper sauce
4 ounces canned baby corn, cut in half

In a large skillet over high heat, bring the water to a boil. Add the shrimp and salt; cook and stir for 3 minutes. Remove from the heat; remove the shrimp with a slotted spoon and set aside. Allow the stock to cool; reserve ¼ cup and set aside.

In a medium bowl, combine all the ingredients *except* the corn and shrimp. Refrigerate for 1 hour. Add the corn and shrimp and stir well.

PER SERVING	KCAL	FATgm	CHOLmg	SODmg
	240	0.8	131	641

Shrimp Enchiladas

When I opened my restaurant, a high-fat version of this appetizer became so popular that we've never taken it off the menu. I decided to create a low-calorie version for this book, and it tastes just as good as the original.

MAKES 4 SERVINGS

1 cup salt-free chicken
  broth
½ pound small shrimp,
  peeled and deveined
½ teaspoon salt
1 tablespoon reduced-
  calorie margarine
½ cup very finely chopped
  onions
2 tablespoons all-purpose
  flour

3 jalapeño peppers,
  chopped
½ teaspoon granulated
  garlic
½ teaspoon dried oregano
  leaves, crushed
½ teaspoon ground cumin
½ cup evaporated skim
  milk
4 corn tortillas

In a medium skillet over high heat, bring *half* of the broth to a boil. Add the shrimp and salt; cook and stir for 8 minutes. Remove from the heat and transfer the shrimp and cooking broth to a bowl; set aside. In the same skillet over high heat, melt the margarine. Add the onions and sauté for 3 minutes. Add the flour; cook and stir for 2 minutes. Stir in the remaining broth, the jalapeños, garlic, oregano and cumin; cook, stirring, for 5 minutes. Add the milk and shrimp with broth. Cook for 8 minutes, or until the sauce thickens, stirring often. Remove from the heat and set aside.

In a small cast-iron skillet over medium heat, brown the tortillas for 1 minute on each side. Place each tortilla on a serving plate and spoon ¼ cup of the shrimp filling into the middle; fold each tortilla in thirds across the filling and turn it seam side down. Serve immediately.

PER SERVING	KCAL	FATgm	CHOLmg	SODmg
	181	3.4	112	497

Sweet-and-Sour Shrimp

MAKES 6 SERVINGS

1½ cups water
1 carrot, peeled and thinly
  sliced
1 tablespoon salt-free
  chicken bouillon
  granules
¼ cup pineapple juice
1 tablespoon balsamic
  vinegar
1 tablespoon lemon juice
2 teaspoons low-sodium soy
  sauce
1 teaspoon liquid sugar
  substitute

½ teaspoon dry mustard
1 cup chopped onions
½ cup chopped celery
½ cup chopped red bell
  pepper
½ cup unsweetened
  pineapple chunks
1 pound shrimp, peeled and
  deveined
½ teaspoon salt
½ teaspoon ground white
  pepper
1 tablespoon cornstarch

In a small saucepan over high heat, bring ½ cup of the water to a boil; add the carrot and cook for 3 to 5 minutes. Drain and set aside, reserving the liquid. Dissolve the bouillon in the reserved liquid and add the next 6 ingredients; stir well and set aside.

Spray the inside of a large skillet with butter-flavored nonstick vegetable cooking spray and place over high heat. Add the onions, celery, bell pepper, pineapple and reserved carrot; sauté for 10 minutes. Remove from the heat and transfer to a bowl.

Spray the same skillet again with cooking spray and place over high heat. Add the shrimp, salt and pepper; cook, stirring, for 5 minutes. Add the sautéed vegetables. Dissolve the cornstarch in the reserved bouillon mixture and pour into the skillet. Cook and stir 5 minutes longer, or until the sauce thickens.

PER SERVING	KCAL	FATgm	CHOLmg	SODmg
	140	1.2	148	426

Curried Shrimp

The flavors of the curry make this dish a real taste bud buster!

MAKES 6 SERVINGS

1½ cups chopped onions
½ cup chopped celery
1 small bell pepper, thinly
 sliced
One 16-ounce can salt-free
 whole tomatoes
1 cup salt-free chicken
 broth
2 teaspoons chili powder
1 teaspoon salt

1 teaspoon granulated
 garlic
½ teaspoon curry powder
¼ teaspoon ground thyme
Pinch of cinnamon
1 pound shrimp, peeled and
 deveined
1 tablespoon lime juice
3 cups hot cooked rice

Spray the inside of a 5-quart Dutch oven with nonstick vegetable cooking spray and place over high heat. Add the onions, celery and bell pepper and sauté for 10 minutes. Add the tomatoes and broth and cook for 5 minutes. Add the next 6 ingredients; cook, stirring, for 10 minutes. Add the shrimp and lime juice. Cook 10 minutes longer, stirring often. Serve over rice.

PER SERVING	KCAL	FATgm	CHOLmg	SODmg
	127	1.4	148	703

Shrimp-Stuffed Eggplant

MAKES 4 SERVINGS

2 small eggplants
2 cups water
1 cup finely chopped onions
½ cup finely chopped green bell pepper
½ cup finely chopped red bell pepper
½ pound small shrimp, peeled and deveined
¼ cup finely chopped green onions

1 teaspoon salt
½ teaspoon ground white pepper
½ teaspoon ground red pepper
1 cup evaporated skim milk
¼ cup fine dry bread crumbs
Paprika

Preheat the oven to 450°F.

Peel the eggplant and cut in half lengthwise. Using a spoon, carefully scoop out the centers, leaving a shell about ¼ inch thick. Finely chop the eggplant pulp and set aside ½ cup. (Use remaining pulp in another recipe.)

Bring the water to a boil over high heat. Add the eggplant shells and cook for 5 minutes. Remove from the heat and drain upside down, then arrange upright in a baking dish and set aside.

Spray the inside of a large skillet with nonstick vegetable cooking spray and place over high heat. Add the onions and bell peppers and sauté for 5 minutes. Add the shrimp and the reserved eggplant pulp, the green onions, salt, white pepper and red pepper. Cook and stir for 5 minutes. Stir in the milk and cook 5 minutes longer.

Fill each eggplant shell with the shrimp mixture; spoon the remaining mixture around the eggplant halves. Sprinkle with bread crumbs and paprika. Bake for 20 minutes, or until heated through and the crumbs start to brown.

PER SERVING	KCAL	FATgm	CHOLmg	SODmg
	163	1.3	113	726

Spicy Shrimp and Rice

MAKES 4 SERVINGS

1 cup finely chopped onions
½ cup finely chopped red
   bell pepper
1½ cups converted rice
1 cup dry white wine
One 10¾-ounce can salt-
   free chicken broth
2 tablespoons lemon juice

2 teaspoons julienned
   lemon rind
2 dried hot chili peppers,
   crushed
½ teaspoon salt
½ cup medium shrimp,
   peeled and deveined
2 tablespoons finely
   chopped green onion

Spray the inside of a medium skillet with butter-flavored nonstick vegetable cooking spray and place over high heat. Add the onions and bell pepper and sauté for 8 minutes. Add the rice; cook, stirring, for 5 minutes. Add the wine and *1 cup* of the broth; continue cooking for 5 minutes. Reduce the heat to medium and add the remaining broth, the lemon juice, lemon rind, chili peppers and salt. Cover and cook for 10 minutes. Add the shrimp and green onion and cook, covered, 10 minutes longer, or until rice is tender and the liquid is absorbed.

PER SERVING	KCAL	FATgm	CHOLmg	SODmg
	385	1.2	111	557

Stuffed Shrimp

Serve these crab-stuffed shrimp as an appetizer.

MAKES 6 SERVINGS

1 teaspoon salt-free lemon-pepper seasoning
¼ teaspoon salt
⅛ teaspoon granulated garlic
⅛ teaspoon ground red pepper
½ pound medium shrimp, peeled, deveined and butterflied
1 cup finely chopped onions
¼ cup finely chopped green bell pepper
¼ cup finely chopped red bell pepper

One-half 10½-ounce can reduced-calorie cream of mushroom soup
1 tablespoon salt-free lemon-pepper seasoning
½ teaspoon salt
½ teaspoon ground red pepper
½ cup evaporated skim milk
1 cup corn flakes, crushed
One 6½-ounce can white crabmeat, picked over
½ cup fine dry bread crumbs

Preheat the oven to 350°F.

Combine the first 4 ingredients in a small bowl and mix well. Sprinkle over the shrimp and set aside. Spray the inside of a large skillet with nonstick vegetable cooking spray and place over high heat. Add the onions and bell peppers and sauté for 5 minutes. Reduce the heat to medium. Add the next 4 ingredients; cook and stir for 5 minutes. Add the skim milk and cook 5 minutes longer. Remove from the heat, add the corn flakes and crabmeat and stir well.

Place equal amounts of the mixture along the center of each shrimp, shaping firmly around the shrimp. Coat each shrimp with bread crumbs and place on a baking dish that has been sprayed with nonstick vegetable cooking spray. Bake for 25 minutes, or until golden brown.

PER SERVING	KCAL	FATgm	CHOLmg	SODmg
	131	1.9	120	630

Sautéed Lemon Shrimp

MAKES 4 SERVINGS

1 teaspoon hickory-smoke-
  flavored seasoning
½ teaspoon salt
½ teaspoon granulated
  garlic
½ teaspoon ground red
  pepper
½ pound large shrimp,
  peeled, deveined and
  butterflied
2 tablespoons salt-free
  chicken bouillon
  granules

1 cup water
2 tablespoons very finely
  chopped onion
2 tablespoons very finely
  chopped red bell pepper
2 tablespoons lemon juice
¼ cup finely chopped green
  onions

Combine the first 4 ingredients in a small bowl; mix well and sprinkle over the shrimp. Dissolve the bouillon granules in the water and set aside.

Spray the inside of a large skillet with nonstick vegetable cooking spray and place over high heat. Add the shrimp and sauté for 3 minutes, stirring constantly. Add the onion and bell pepper and sauté for 5 minutes. Stir in the dissolved bouillon and cook 3 minutes longer. Add the lemon juice and cook 1 minute more. Remove from the heat, add the green onions and let stand 2 minutes before serving.

PER SERVING	KCAL	FATgm	CHOLmg	SODmg
	63	0.7	111	374

Shrimp Sauce Piquant

MAKES 6 SERVINGS

2 cups chopped onions
1/2 cup chopped green bell
    pepper
1/4 cup chopped celery
One 14 1/2-ounce can salt-
    free whole tomatoes
3 tablespoons tomato paste
2 cups salt-free chicken
    broth
1 bay leaf
1 tablespoon low-sodium
    Worcestershire sauce
1 teaspoon brown sugar

1/2 teaspoon granulated
    garlic
1/2 teaspoon dried basil,
    crushed
1/2 teaspoon salt
1/2 teaspoon ground red
    pepper
1 pound medium shrimp,
    peeled and deveined
1/4 cup finely chopped green
    onions
1/4 cup finely chopped fresh
    parsley

Spray the inside of a 5-quart Dutch oven with nonstick vegetable cooking spray and place over high heat. Add the onions, bell pepper and celery and sauté for 8 minutes. Add the tomatoes, tomato paste, broth and bay leaf; cook, stirring, for 20 minutes. Add the next 6 ingredients; cover and cook for 5 minutes. Add the shrimp, green onions and parsley. Reduce the heat to medium and cook, covered, 10 minutes longer.

PER SERVING	KCAL	FATgm	CHOLmg	SODmg
	114	1.2	148	355

Grilled Shrimp with Brown Rice Pilaf

I put this dish on my menu in the restaurant for a few days, and when I took it off, there were lots of requests to put it back!

MAKES 5 SERVINGS

1 tablespoon salt-free
    lemon-pepper
    seasoning
1 teaspoon salt
1 teaspoon onion powder
1 teaspoon granulated
    garlic
1 teaspoon chili powder
½ teaspoon ground white
    pepper

1 pound large shrimp,
    peeled and deveined
½ cup finely chopped
    onions
½ cup finely chopped green
    bell pepper
½ cup finely chopped red
    bell pepper
4 cups shrimp stock or
    water
1 cup brown rice

Preheat a charcoal or gas grill.

In a small bowl, combine the first 6 ingredients. Mix well and reserve *1 tablespoon*. Sprinkle the remaining seasoning mix over the shrimp. Thread the shrimp onto 5 skewers and place on the hot grill. Cook for 4 minutes on each side; set aside and keep warm.

Spray the inside of a 5-quart Dutch oven with nonstick vegetable cooking spray and place over high heat. Add the onions and bell peppers and sauté for 5 minutes. Stir in the stock, the reserved seasoning and the rice and cook for 10 minutes. Reduce the heat, cover and simmer for another 20 minutes, stirring often.

PER SERVING	KCAL	FATgm	CHOLmg	SODmg
	152	1.5	177	606

Shrimp-Stuffed Cucumber Baskets

This is a delicious appetizer to serve for those special parties. Your friends will really be impressed!

MAKES 8 APPETIZER SERVINGS

2 slices bread (40 calories per slice)
3 medium cucumbers, cut into 1-inch slices (16 slices)
½ pound small shrimp, peeled and deveined
1 jalapeño pepper, minced
⅓ cup very finely chopped onions
⅓ cup very finely chopped red bell pepper
½ teaspoon salt-free lemon-pepper seasoning
¼ teaspoon salt
¼ teaspoon ground white pepper
⅓ cup water
2 tablespoons reduced-calorie soft-style cream cheese
1 tablespoon lemon juice
1 tablespoon finely chopped fresh parsley

Place the bread in a food processor and process into crumbs; set aside. Carefully scoop out the center of each cucumber slice, leaving about a ⅛-inch shell; discard the seeds and set the cucumbers aside.

Spray the inside of a large skillet with nonstick vegetable cooking spray and place over high heat. Add the shrimp and next 6 ingredients and sauté for 3 minutes. Stir in the water and cook 2 minutes longer. Remove the skillet from the heat and set aside 16 of the shrimp. Chop the remaining shrimp and return to the skillet along with the bread crumbs, cream cheese and lemon juice, stirring well. Spoon equal amounts of the shrimp mixture into each cucumber and top each with 1 shrimp. Sprinkle with parsley and place 2 cucumbers on each plate.

PER SERVING	KCAL	FATgm	CHOLmg	SODmg
	59	0.5	55	155

Baked Oysters with Shrimp

*T*his blend of succulent oysters with fresh shrimp, along with the seasonings, makes for a delicious dish you'll want to prepare often.

MAKES 4 SERVINGS

1 tablespoon reduced-
  calorie margarine
1 tablespoon all-purpose
  flour
1 cup chopped onions
¼ cup chopped celery
¼ cup chopped green bell
  pepper
½ pound small shrimp,
  peeled and deveined
1 cup thinly sliced
  mushrooms
½ cup red wine
¼ cup liquid from oysters
½ teaspoon ground white
  pepper

½ teaspoon Italian
  seasoning
¼ teaspoon salt
¼ cup finely chopped green
  onions
1 tablespoon chopped
  pimiento
Rock salt
8 oysters, shucked
2 slices bread (40 calories
  per slice), made into
  crumbs
¼ cup freshly grated
  Parmesan cheese
Paprika

Preheat the oven to 400°F.

Melt the margarine in a medium skillet over medium heat. Add the flour; cook and stir for 1 minute. Add the onions, celery and bell pepper; cook, stirring, for 10 minutes. Add the next 7 ingredients. Cook and stir for 10 minutes. Add the green onions and pimiento and cook 5 minutes longer. Remove from the heat and set aside.

Place enough rock salt on a baking sheet to cover the bottom. Arrange 4 glass oyster shells in the salt and place 2 oysters in each shell. Spoon equal portions of the shrimp mixture over the oysters. Add the cheese and bread crumbs, sprinkle with paprika and bake for 20 minutes.

PER SERVING	KCAL	FATgm	CHOLmg	SODmg
	167	3.6	126	311

Spicy Louisiana Oysters

1 cup finely chopped onions
1 cup thinly sliced fresh
    mushrooms
1/2 cup finely chopped green
    bell pepper
3 tablespoons tomato paste
One 6-ounce can tomato
    juice
1 cup stewed tomatoes
1 1/2 teaspoons chopped
    jalapeño pepper
1 cup salt-free chicken
    broth

1/2 cup liquid from oysters
1 teaspoon brown sugar
1 teaspoon dried basil
    leaves, crushed
1 pint fresh oysters,
    shucked
1 tablespoon lemon juice
1/4 cup finely chopped green
    onions
1/4 cup finely chopped fresh
    parsley

Spray the inside of a large skillet with butter-flavored nonstick vegetable cooking spray and place over high heat. Add the onions, mushrooms and bell pepper and sauté for 5 minutes. Stir the tomato paste into the tomato juice and add to the skillet along with the stewed tomatoes and jalapeño. Cook, stirring, for 10 minutes. Reduce the heat to medium and add the broth, oyster liquid, sugar and basil. Cook, covered, for 10 minutes, stirring often. Add all the remaining ingredients, stirring well. Reduce the heat to a simmer and cook, covered, 5 minutes longer, or until the edges of the oysters start to curl.

PER SERVING	KCAL	FATgm	CHOLmg	SODmg
	146	3.9	69	322

Slipper Lobsters in Cream Sauce

Slipper lobsters are strange-looking creatures that are closer to the size of shrimp than to lobsters. If they're not available, substitute shrimp.

MAKES 4 SERVINGS

1 cup chopped onions
1 roasted green bell pepper
(page 220), diced
1 roasted red bell pepper,
diced
½ teaspoon granulated
garlic
½ teaspoon ground white
pepper
½ teaspoon dried basil
leaves, crushed
½ teaspoon paprika

¼ teaspoon salt
1 tablespoon all-purpose
flour
2 teaspoons salt-free
chicken bouillon
granules
1 cup water
1 pound slipper lobsters,
peeled and skinned
1 cup evaporated skim milk
2 teaspoons dry sherry
2 cups hot cooked rice

Spray the inside of a large skillet with nonstick vegetable cooking spray and place over high heat. Add the onions and roasted bell peppers and sauté for 5 minutes. Add the next 5 ingredients. Dissolve the flour and bouillon granules in the water and add to the skillet. Reduce the heat to medium and cook, stirring, for 5 minutes.

Add the lobsters and cook for 5 minutes. Stir in the milk and cook for 3 minutes. Stir in the sherry and cook 1 minute longer. Serve over rice.

PER SERVING	KCAL	FATgm	CHOLmg	SODmg
	142	0.9	81	679

Scallops Marinara

If scallops are not available in your area, substitute shrimp. Either way, this is a great tasting, hearty meal. Serve with hot cooked rice or pasta.

MAKES 4 SERVINGS

1 cup chopped onions
½ cup chopped green bell pepper
One 16-ounce can salt-free whole tomatoes, chopped
2 tablespoons tomato paste
1 cup salt-free chicken broth
½ teaspoon salt

½ teaspoon sugar
½ teaspoon granulated garlic
½ teaspoon ground white pepper
½ teaspoon dried basil leaves, crushed
1 pound sea scallops, cut ½-inch thick

Spray the inside of a large skillet with nonstick vegetable cooking spray and place over high heat. Add the onions and bell pepper and sauté for 5 minutes. Add the tomatoes (with their juice) and tomato paste; cook, stirring for 10 minutes. Add the next 6 ingredients. Cook and stir for 15 minutes. Add the scallops and cook 5 minutes longer. Do not overcook.

PER SERVING	KCAL	FATgm	CHOLmg	SODmg
	128	1.1	37	434

FISH

Swordfish with Tarragon and Vermouth

1½ teaspoons salt
1 teaspoon salt-free lemon-pepper seasoning
1 teaspoon ground tarragon
1 teaspoon ground red pepper
1½ pounds swordfish fillets or any firm, white-fleshed fish, cut ¼ inch thick

1 carrot, cut into julienne strips
1 zucchini, cut into julienne strips
1 yellow squash, cut into julienne strips
1 onion, thinly sliced and separated into rings
3 tablespoons dry vermouth

Preheat the oven to 375°F.

In a small bowl, combine the salt, lemon-pepper seasoning, tarragon and red pepper. Mix well and reserve *1 teaspoon* for later use. Sprinkle the remaining seasoning mix over both sides of the fish and set aside. Cut a piece of foil about 3 feet long. Place the foil on a baking sheet and spray with nonstick vegetable cooking spray. Arrange the fillets on the foil and place the carrots, zucchini and squash around them. Spoon the vermouth over the fish. Carefully seal all ends of the foil tightly. Place in the oven and bake for 30 minutes. To serve, remove the foil, cut into serving pieces and sprinkle with the remaining seasoning mix.

PER SERVING	KCAL	FATgm	CHOLmg	SODmg
	155	4.8	3	514

Rainbow Trout with Crab Stuffing

1 teaspoon salt
1 teaspoon granulated
　garlic
1 teaspoon ground white
　pepper
1 teaspoon chili powder
¼ teaspoon ground thyme
¼ teaspoon dried oregano
　leaves, crushed
4 rainbow trout, boned
½ cup finely chopped
　onions
½ cup finely chopped green
　bell pepper

½ cup finely chopped red
　bell pepper
1 cup water
2 slices bread (40 calories
　per slice), toasted and
　cut into ¼-inch cubes
½ cup evaporated skim
　milk
1 tablespoon lemon juice
One 6½-ounce can white
　crabmeat, picked over

Preheat the broiler.

Combine the first 6 ingredients in a small bowl. Mix well and reserve *1 tablespoon* for later use. Sprinkle the remaining seasoning mix over both sides of the fish and set aside. Spray the inside of a large skillet with butter-flavored nonstick vegetable cooking spray and place over high heat. Add the onions and bell peppers and sauté for 5 minutes. Stir in the water and the reserved seasoning mix. Add the bread cubes, milk and lemon juice, stirring well. Remove from the heat and carefully fold in the crabmeat; let cool to the touch.

Spoon ½ *cup* of the stuffing mix into the cavity of each fish, pressing the edges of the cavity together to prevent it from falling out. Place the fish on a broiler pan that has been sprayed with nonstick vegetable cooking spray. Place in the broiler about 6 inches from the heat and broil for 10 minutes.

PER SERVING	KCAL	FATgm	CHOLmg	SODmg
	257	6.2	127	786

Grilled Flounder with Crawfish Sauce

If crawfish are not available, substitute shrimp.

⅛ teaspoon salt
⅛ teaspoon ground white
    pepper
⅛ teaspoon dried oregano
    leaves, crushed
⅛ teaspoon ground thyme
2 flounder fillets (about 3
    ounces each)
1 teaspoon lemon juice

1½ ounces crawfish tails,
    peeled and deveined
½ cup seafood stock or
    water
½ cup evaporated skim
    milk
1 teaspoon paprika
½ teaspoon hot pepper
    sauce

Preheat a charcoal or gas grill.

TO PREPARE FISH: Mix together the first 4 ingredients. Sprinkle *half* of the seasoning mix over both sides of the fish; reserve the remainder for later use. Place the fish on the hot grill and cook for 4 minutes on each side, carefully turning with a spatula. Transfer to a warm plate, then top each fillet with lemon juice. Keep warm.

TO PREPARE SAUCE: In a medium skillet over medium heat, cook the crawfish and stock, stirring often, for 3 minutes. Remove from the heat and let cool to the touch. Reserve 6 crawfish tails and set aside. Place the remaining crawfish in a food processor and process until smooth. Return to the skillet over medium heat along with milk, paprika, hot sauce and reserved seasoning mix.

Cook for 5 minutes, or until the sauce thickens, stirring constantly. Remove from the heat and spoon equal amounts of the sauce in center of 2 individual plates. Place a fish fillet over the sauce, then garnish each plate with 3 of the reserved crawfish tails.

PER SERVING	KCAL	FATgm	CHOLmg	SODmg
	178	1.9	98	307

Grilled Pompano

Pompano is one of our favorite catches from the Gulf of Mexico. If you can't find it, substitute flounder or any white fish fillets.

MAKES 4 SERVINGS

½ teaspoon paprika
¼ teaspoon salt
¼ teaspoon ground white
    pepper
¼ teaspoon ground thyme

¼ teaspoon dried oregano
    leaves, crushed
¼ teaspoon ground red
    pepper
1 pound pompano fillets

Combine the first 6 ingredients in a small bowl. Mix well and sprinkle over the fish. Place a cast-iron griddle over medium heat and heat until very hot. Grill each fillet, skin side down, for 4 minutes. Turn, then grill an additional 3 minutes, or until the fish flakes easily with a fork.

PER SERVING	KCAL	FATgm	CHOLmg	SODmg
	241	13.8	72	209

Panfried Salmon Patties

My mother's salmon patties are a family favorite. Top them with the delicious cheese sauce on page 286.

MAKES 12 PATTIES

3 cups water
1 small potato, peeled and cubed
One 14 ¾-ounce can pink salmon, drained and picked over
¼ cup egg substitute
¼ cup very finely chopped onion

2 tablespoons very finely chopped red bell pepper
1 tablespoon very finely chopped fresh parsley
½ teaspoon ground red pepper
¼ cup all-purpose flour

In a medium saucepan over high heat, bring the water to a boil. Add the potato and boil for 10 minutes, or until tender. Drain and let cool to the touch, then mash the potato with a fork; set aside.

In a large bowl, combine the salmon, egg substitute, onion, bell pepper, parsley, red pepper and potato; stir well. Divide the mixture into 12 pieces and shape into 3-inch patties. Place the flour on a plate, then dredge the patties through it.

Spray the inside of a large skillet with nonstick vegetable cooking spray and place over medium heat. Place the patties in the skillet and cook for 1 minute on each side. Spray the skillet again with cooking spray; cook the patties 2 minutes longer, or until golden brown, turning often to prevent burning.

PER PATTY	KCAL	FATgm	CHOLmg	SODmg
	65	2	0	169

Grilled Salmon with Corn Salsa

MAKES 4 SERVINGS

½ teaspoon salt
¼ teaspoon granulated
  garlic
¼ teaspoon dried basil
  leaves, crushed

1 pound salmon fillets, cut
  ¾ inch thick
1 cup Corn Salsa
  (page 282)

Preheat a charcoal or gas grill.

Combine the salt, garlic and basil and sprinkle over both sides of the fish. Spray the fish on both sides with nonstick vegetable cooking spray. Grill 6 inches from the heat for 3 minutes on each side, or until the fish flakes easily with a fork. Transfer to a warm plate and top each fillet with 2 tablespoons of corn salsa.

PER SERVING	KCAL	FATgm	CHOLmg	SODmg
	210	8.6	56	311

Steamed Salmon with Sour Cream Dressing

MAKES 4 SERVINGS

½ teaspoon hickory-smoke-flavored salt
½ teaspoon onion powder
½ teaspoon granulated garlic
½ teaspoon ground white pepper
1 pound salmon steaks, cut ¾ inch thick
1½ cups water
1 tablespoon chopped onion
2 teaspoons finely chopped fresh parsley

½ cup fat-free sour cream
½ cup fat-free mayonnaise
¼ cup evaporated skim milk
2 tablespoons minced red onion
1 tablespoon minced red bell pepper
1 tablespoon Dijon mustard
1 teaspoon hot pepper sauce

In a small bowl, combine the first 4 ingredients. Mix well and sprinkle over both sides of the fish. Place the water in a steamer and bring to a boil over high heat. Add the fish, onion and parsley. Cover and steam for 5 to 8 minutes. Remove from the heat, transfer to a plate and keep warm.

In a medium bowl, combine all the remaining ingredients. Mix well and spoon over the fish.

PER SERVING OF FISH	KCAL	FATgm	CHOLmg	SODmg
	213	8.6	56.03	67

PER TABLESPOON OF SAUCE	KCAL	FATgm	CHOLmg	SODmg
	5	0	0	15

Orange Roughy with Champagne Sauce

If orange roughy is not available in your area, substitute any other firm fish.

MAKES 4 SERVINGS

1 tablespoon low-sodium
    soy sauce
1 teaspoon chili powder
1/2 teaspoon salt
1/2 teaspoon granulated
    garlic
1/2 teaspoon ground red
    pepper
1 pound orange roughy
    fillets or any firm,
    white-fleshed fish
1 cup thinly sliced
    mushrooms

1/2 medium onion, thinly
    sliced and separated
    into rings
1/2 medium green bell
    pepper, thinly sliced
1/2 medium red bell pepper,
    thinly sliced
1/2 cup salt-free chicken
    broth
1/2 cup champagne

Sprinkle the soy sauce, chili powder, salt, garlic and red pepper over both sides of the fish. Spray the inside of a large skillet with nonstick vegetable cooking spray and place over high heat. Add the fish and cook for 4 minutes on each side, turning often to prevent burning. Transfer the fish to a platter and keep warm. Spray the same skillet again with cooking spray and place over high heat. Add the mushrooms, onion and bell peppers; cook, stirring, for 5 minutes. Remove from the heat and spoon on top of the fish. To the same skillet, add the broth and champagne. Cook for 5 minutes, or until the liquid is reduced by half; spoon over the fish.

PER SERVING	KCAL	FATgm	CHOLmg	SODmg
	171	1.9	131	499

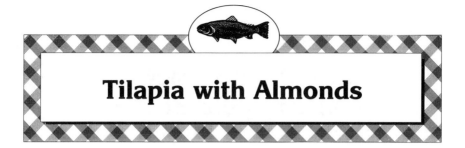

Tilapia with Almonds

If tilapia is not available, substitute your favorite fish. The toasted almonds will turn any fish into a taste-tempting dish.

MAKES 4 SERVINGS

¼ cup slivered almonds
2 cups corn flakes, coarsely crushed
1 teaspoon onion powder
½ teaspoon salt
½ teaspoon granulated garlic

½ teaspoon ground red pepper
1 pound tilapia fillets or any firm, white-fleshed fish
¼ cup fat-free Italian dressing
½ teaspoon paprika

Preheat the oven to 450°F.

Place the almonds and corn flakes on a baking sheet and bake for 5 minutes, or until the almonds are crisp. Remove from the oven and set aside. In a small bowl, combine the next 4 ingredients; mix well and sprinkle over the fish. Pour on the dressing and refrigerate for 20 minutes. Lightly press each fillet in the almond and corn flake mixture. Place the fillets on a baking sheet and sprinkle with paprika. Bake for 10 to 12 minutes, or until the fish flakes easily with a fork.

PER SERVING	KCAL	FATgm	CHOLmg	SODmg
	221	5.6	77	505

Poached Amberjack with Raspberry Vinegar Sauce

MAKES 4 SERVINGS

6 cups water
10 black peppercorns
3 ribs celery
2 bay leaves
1 large unpeeled onion,
    quartered
1 large carrot, cut into 2-
    inch slices
1 large lemon, quartered
1 cup shrimp peelings
1 pound amberjack fillets
2 teaspoons salt
2 teaspoons hot pepper
    sauce

FOR THE SAUCE

1 tablespoon reduced-
    calorie margarine
1 tablespoon all-purpose
    flour
2 tablespoons raspberry
    vinegar
1 tablespoon very finely
    chopped fresh parsley
1 teaspoon garlic powder
1 teaspoon onion powder

TO PREPARE FISH: In a 5-quart Dutch oven over high heat, bring the water to a boil. Add the next 7 ingredients and cook for 30 minutes. Remove from the heat and strain, reserving 3 cups of the stock and discarding the solids. In a large skillet over medium heat, add the fish, salt and hot pepper sauce to *2 cups* of the stock. Reduce the heat to a simmer and cook, covered, for 10 minutes, or until the fish flakes easily with a fork. Remove from the heat and transfer the fish to a platter; keep warm.

TO PREPARE SAUCE: Melt the margarine in a medium skillet over medium heat. Add the flour and cook, stirring, for 1 minute. Add the remaining 1 cup stock, and all the remaining ingredients; cook and stir for 5 minutes. Remove from the heat and spoon the sauce over the fish.

PER SERVING	KCAL	FATgm	CHOLmg	SODmg
	268	5.8	157	306

74

Baked Amberjack

1 tablespoon granulated
    garlic
1 tablespoon onion powder
1 teaspoon paprika
¼ teaspoon salt
¼ teaspoon ground white
    pepper
1 pound amberjack fillets or
    any firm, white-fleshed
    fish, cut ½ inch thick
2 tablespoons prepared
    mustard

2 tablespoons salt-free
    chicken broth
1 tablespoon lemon juice
2 teaspoons prepared
    horseradish
2 tablespoons very finely
    chopped green onion
1 tablespoon very finely
    chopped fresh parsley

Preheat the oven to 350°F.

In a small bowl, combine the first 5 ingredients; mix well and sprinkle over both sides of the fish. In a pie plate, mix together the mustard, broth, lemon juice and horseradish. Dredge each fillet through the mustard mixture, then place in a 9-inch-square baking dish that has been sprayed with nonstick vegetable cooking spray. Cover and bake for 20 minutes, or until the fish flakes easily with a fork. Remove the fish with a spatula and place on a warm platter. Reserve the liquid.

In a small skillet over high heat, bring the reserved liquid to a boil. Add the green onion and parsley and cook until the liquid is reduced by half. Remove from the heat and spoon over the fish.

PER SERVING	KCAL	FATgm	CHOLmg	SODmg
	136	1.9	41	226

Grilled Amberjack with Spinach Sauce

Anisette is a licorice-flavored liqueur.

Makes 4 servings

4 cups water
10 ounces fresh spinach
1 tablespoon reduced-
    calorie margarine
1 cup finely chopped onions
¼ cup finely chopped red
    bell pepper
2 tablespoons all-purpose
    flour
1½ cups evaporated skim
    milk
1 teaspoon anisette

¾ teaspoon salt
¾ teaspoon ground red
    pepper
½ teaspoon granulated
    garlic
½ teaspoon onion powder
½ teaspoon hickory-smoke-
    flavored seasoning
1 pound amberjack fillets or
    any firm, white-fleshed
    fish, cut ¼ inch thick

Preheat a charcoal or gas grill.

In a large saucepan, bring the water to a boil over high heat. Remove the stems and wash the spinach thoroughly. Add to the boiling water and cook for 10 minutes; drain and set aside. Melt the margarine in a heavy skillet over high heat. Add the onions and bell pepper and sauté for 2 minutes. Add the flour and cook, stirring, for 1 minute. Reduce the heat to medium and add the milk, anisette, ¼ teaspoon of the salt and ¼ teaspoon of the red pepper. Cook for 8 minutes, stirring often. Add the cooked spinach and cook 10 minutes longer. Remove from the heat and keep warm.

Combine the garlic, onion powder, hickory seasoning, and remaining salt and red pepper in a small bowl; mix well and sprinkle over both sides of the fish. Place the fish on the hot grill and cook for 5 to 8 minutes on each side; keep warm. Spoon the spinach sauce on a platter and top with the grilled fish.

PER SERVING	KCAL	FATgm	CHOLmg	SODmg
	263	3.8	81	687

Monkfish Florentine

The analysis for this recipe includes all ingredients except *the monkfish.*

MAKES 4 SERVINGS

1 teaspoon dried dillweed
½ teaspoon salt
¼ teaspoon granulated
   garlic
¼ teaspoon ground white
   pepper
¼ teaspoon paprika
4 monkfish fillets (about 4
   ounces each) or any
   firm, white-fleshed fish,
   cut in half lengthwise

FOR THE STUFFING
5 ounces fresh spinach
½ cup finely chopped
   onions

½ cup finely chopped red
   bell pepper
¼ teaspoon dried dillweed
¼ teaspoon salt
⅛ teaspoon garlic powder
2 slices bread (40 calories
   per slice), toasted and
   finely crumbled
Two ¾-ounce slices
   reduced-fat American
   cheese product, diced
2 tablespoons egg
   substitute

Preheat the broiler.

Combine the first 5 ingredients in a small bowl. Mix well and sprinkle over both sides of the fish. Spray a baking sheet with nonstick vegetable cooking spray. Arrange the fish on the baking sheet and broil for 5 minutes on each side. Remove from the heat and keep warm.

Rinse the spinach under cold water. Remove the stems and discard. Chop the spinach and set aside. Spray the inside of a medium skillet with nonstick vegetable cooking spray and place over medium heat. Add the onions and bell pepper and sauté for 3 minutes. Add the spinach, dill, salt and garlic powder; cook 3 minutes longer, stirring often. Remove from the heat and add the bread crumbs, cheese and egg substitute, stirring well. Spoon equal amounts of the stuffing over each fillet, then return to the broiler for 3 minutes, or until heated through.

PER SERVING	KCAL	FATgm	CHOLmg	SODmg
	82	2.5	0	675

Monkfish Medallions with Wine-Cream Sauce

Monkfish is more popular in Europe than in North America, but the meat has a delicious, rich flavor. The fish itself is very ugly, with a huge head, so only the tail section is eaten.

MAKES 4 SERVINGS

1 pound monkfish fillets or any firm, white-fleshed fish
1 teaspoon dried dillweed
½ teaspoon salt
¼ teaspoon ground white pepper
¼ teaspoon paprika
⅓ cup all-purpose flour

FOR THE SAUCE
1 tablespoon reduced-calorie margarine

1 tablespoon all-purpose flour
1 cup evaporated skim milk
2 tablespoons finely chopped green onion
⅛ teaspoon salt
⅛ teaspoon ground white pepper
¼ cup white wine
One ¾-ounce slice reduced-fat American cheese product, diced

Pound the fillets to a ⅛-inch thickness, then cut into medallions 2 inches in diameter. Combine the dill, salt, white pepper and paprika and sprinkle over both sides of the fish. Dredge the fish in the flour and set aside. Spray the inside of a medium skillet with nonstick vegetable cooking spray and place over medium heat. Cook the fillets for 2 minutes on each side. Transfer to a platter and keep warm.

Meanwhile, melt the margarine in a small skillet over medium heat. Add the flour and cook, stirring, for 1 minute. Add the milk, green onion, salt and pepper; cook and stir for 1 minute. Reduce the heat and add the wine and cheese; cook, stirring, 1 minute longer. Remove from the heat and spoon the sauce over the fish.

PER SERVING	KCAL	FATgm	CHOLmg	SODmg
	125	2.7	3	528

Crispy Spicy Catfish

I *use tater crisps to make this dish, but you can use any kind of low-fat or fat-free potato chip.*

MAKES 4 SERVINGS

½ ounce fat-free potato
    chips, crushed
½ ounce corn flakes,
    crushed
1 teaspoon dried basil
    leaves, crushed
½ teaspoon granulated
    garlic
½ teaspoon ground thyme

½ teaspoon ground oregano
½ teaspoon salt
½ teaspoon chili powder
½ teaspoon ground red
    pepper
1 pound catfish fillets or
    any firm, white-fleshed
    fish
2 egg whites, beaten

Preheat the oven to 375°F.

Mix together the first 6 ingredients and place on a plate; set aside. Sprinkle the salt, chili powder and red pepper over both sides of the fish. Dip each fillet in egg white, then dredge in the corn flake mixture. Place the fish on a baking sheet that has been sprayed with nonstick vegetable cooking spray. Bake for 20 minutes, or until the fish flakes easily with a fork.

PER SERVING	KCAL	FATgm	CHOLmg	SODmg
	17	3	6	434

Oven-Fried Catfish

MAKES 4 SERVINGS

1½ teaspoons paprika
1 teaspoon salt
1 teaspoon granulated
   garlic
½ teaspoon ground white
   pepper
½ teaspoon ground red
   pepper

1 pound catfish fillets or
   any firm, white-fleshed
   fish
½ cup buttermilk
1 tablespoon lemon juice
2 cups corn flakes, coarsely
   crushed

Preheat the oven to 450°F.

In a small bowl, mix together ½ teaspoon of the paprika, the salt, garlic, white pepper and red pepper and sprinkle over both sides of the fish.

In a medium bowl, mix together the buttermilk and lemon juice. Dip each fillet in the milk, then dredge in the corn flakes. Spray a baking sheet with nonstick vegetable cooking spray. Arrange the fillets about 1 inch apart on the baking sheet. Sprinkle the remaining paprika over the fillets and bake for 20 minutes, or until the fish flakes easily with a fork.

PER SERVING	KCAL	FATgm	CHOLmg	SODmg
	202	1.8	132	613

Catfish Florentine

My granddaughter insists this dish tastes too good to have spinach in it.

MAKES 4 SERVINGS

1 pound fresh spinach
1 cup finely chopped onions
1 cup finely chopped celery
¼ cup finely chopped red
    bell pepper
2 teaspoons granulated
    garlic
1 teaspoon chili powder
½ teaspoon salt
½ teaspoon ground white
    pepper

½ teaspoon ground oregano
½ teaspoon ground thyme
½ teaspoon paprika
½ teaspoon ground red
    pepper
4 catfish fillets (about 5
    ounces each) or any
    firm, white-fleshed fish
½ cup shredded reduced-fat
    Cheddar-Jack cheese

Preheat the oven to 375°F.

Rinse the spinach under cold water, remove the stems and set aside. Spray the inside of a medium skillet with butter-flavored nonstick vegetable cooking spray and place over high heat. Add the onions, celery and bell pepper and sauté for 5 minutes. Add the spinach leaves and cook, stirring, 5 minutes longer. Remove from the heat and set aside.

In a small bowl, combine all the dry seasonings. Mix well and sprinkle on both sides of the fish. Spread *2 tablespoons* of the spinach mixture across the middle of each fillet, then roll up, jelly-roll fashion.

Spoon the remaining spinach mixture into a 9-inch-square baking dish. Add the fish fillets and spray with butter-flavored cooking spray. Cover with aluminum foil and bake for 25 minutes. Uncover, sprinkle with the cheese and bake 5 minutes longer, or until the fish flakes easily with a fork and the cheese is melted.

PER SERVING	KCAL	FATgm	CHOLmg	SODmg
	248	5	77	553

Alligator Stir-fry

I created this dish for the Louisiana Agricultural Department and served it at a New Orleans food show. We kept a long line of people waiting for a taste. Everyone liked it so much that I began to recognize a few faces in line for seconds, and even thirds.

MAKES 4 SERVINGS

1 pound alligator meat, cut into ¼-inch strips
¼ teaspoon salt
½ teaspoon ground white pepper
½ teaspoon ground red pepper
½ teaspoon chili powder
3 tablespoons low-sodium soy sauce
1 tablespoon low-sodium Worcestershire sauce
1 tablespoon cornstarch
2 cups beef stock or water
1 small zucchini, cut into julienne strips
1 small squash, cut into julienne strips
½ medium onion, thinly sliced
1 cup fresh broccoli florets
1 cup fresh cauliflowerettes
4 thinly sliced red bell pepper rings

Spray the inside of a large skillet with nonstick vegetable cooking spray and place over high heat. Add the meat and sauté for 5 minutes. Add the next 6 ingredients and cook for 10 minutes, stirring often. Dissolve the cornstarch in the stock and add to the skillet along with all the remaining ingredients, stirring well. Cook 10 minutes longer, or until the sauce thickens, stirring occasionally.

PER SERVING	KCAL	FATgm	CHOLmg	SODmg
	155	2	52	385

CHICKEN AND TURKEY

No-Fuss Baked Chicken

MAKES 6 SERVINGS

1 teaspoon salt
½ teaspoon ground white
  pepper
½ teaspoon dried basil
  leaves, crushed
½ teaspoon ground thyme
One 3-pound chicken,
  skinned, boned and cut
  into serving pieces
1 tomato, peeled, seeded
  and chopped
1½ cups coarsely chopped
  onions

½ cup coarsely chopped
  celery
½ cup coarsely chopped
  bell pepper
2 tablespoons low-sodium
  Worcestershire sauce
¼ cup tomato paste
1½ cups salt-free chicken
  broth
3 tablespoons lemon juice

Preheat the oven to 450°F.

Sprinkle the salt, white pepper, basil and thyme over the chicken. Spray the inside of a roasting pan with butter-flavored nonstick vegetable cooking spray. Place the chicken in the pan, along with the chopped vegetables. Add the Worcestershire sauce. Mix the tomato paste, broth and lemon juice and pour over the chicken. Cover with aluminum foil and bake for 30 minutes.

PER SERVING	KCAL	FATgm	CHOLmg	SODmg
	203	6.5	86	417

Crispy Oven-Fried Chicken

This dish gets the crispy, crunchy flavor of fried chicken from crushed corn flakes. Now you can enjoy the taste of old-fashioned fried chicken—without the old-fashioned fat!

MAKES 3 SERVINGS

1 teaspoon paprika	3 skinned and boned
½ teaspoon garlic powder	chicken breast halves
⅛ teaspoon ground thyme	(about 5 ounces each)
⅛ teaspoon ground red	⅓ cup buttermilk
pepper	½ cup crushed corn flakes

Preheat the oven to 350°F.

In a small bowl, combine the paprika, garlic powder, thyme and red pepper; mix well and sprinkle over both sides of the chicken; set aside. Pour the buttermilk into a small bowl. Put the corn flakes in a plastic bag. Dip the chicken in the buttermilk, then drop into the corn flakes, shaking the bag to coat the chicken.

Spray the inside of an 8-inch-square baking dish with nonstick vegetable cooking spray. Arrange the chicken in the dish and bake for 45 minutes, or until it is tender and the coating is crisp.

PER SERVING	KCAL	FATgm	CHOLmg	SODmg
	264	5.4	121	180

Lemon Baked Chicken

MAKES 6 SERVINGS

1 tablespoon salt-free
    lemon-pepper
    seasoning
1 teaspoon paprika
½ teaspoon salt
½ teaspoon ground red
    pepper
One 2½-to-3-pound
    chicken, skin and fat
    removed

1 small onion, cut in half
1 large lemon, quartered
½ green bell pepper
1 large potato, peeled and
    cut into ½-inch cubes

Preheat the oven to 350°F.

Combine the lemon-pepper seasoning, paprika, salt and red pepper and sprinkle over the chicken and inside the cavity. Put the onion, *half* of the lemon and the bell pepper inside the cavity of the chicken. Squeeze the remaining lemon over the chicken. Spray the inside of a 9-inch-square baking dish with butter-flavored nonstick vegetable cooking spray. Place the chicken in the dish and arrange the potatoes around it. Cover and bake for 30 minutes. Uncover and bake 30 minutes longer. Remove the onion, lemon and bell pepper from the cavity before serving.

PER SERVING	KCAL	FATgm	CHOLmg	SODmg
	272	6.5	129	284

Honey Roasted Chicken

This dish has a very light and delicate sweetness. Serve it with Baked Texas Rice (page 272) and Spicy Glazed Carrots (page 207).

Makes 4 servings

One 2½-pound chicken,
    skin and fat removed
½ teaspoon salt
¼ teaspoon granulated
    garlic
¼ teaspoon dried basil
    leaves, crushed
¼ teaspoon dried oregano
    leaves, crushed
¼ teaspoon ground cumin

¼ teaspoon chili powder
3 tablespoons honey
2 tablespoons Dijon
    mustard
2 tablespoons balsamic
    vinegar
¼ cup finely chopped onion
¼ cup finely chopped red
    bell pepper
1 teaspoon cornstarch

Preheat the oven to 450°F.

Cut the chicken in half lengthwise. Remove the breast bone and discard. Combine the next 6 ingredients in a small bowl; mix well and sprinkle over both sides of the chicken; set aside. In a small bowl, combine the honey, mustard and vinegar and mix well. Using a pastry brush, brush *half* of the mixture over the chicken; reserve the remaining mixture. Place the chicken in a 9-inch-square baking dish that has been sprayed with nonstick vegetable cooking spray. Cover and bake for 25 minutes. Uncover and bake 15 minutes longer. Remove from the heat; drain the pan juices and reserve.

Spray the inside of a medium skillet with nonstick vegetable cooking spray and place over medium heat. Add the onion and bell pepper and sauté for 3 minutes. Dissolve the cornstarch in the reserved pan juices and add to the skillet, along with the reserved honey mixture. Cook and stir 3 minutes longer, or until the sauce thickens. Remove from the heat and spoon the sauce over the chicken.

PER SERVING	KCAL	FATgm	CHOLmg	SODmg
	330	10	129	346

Sweet-and-Sour Chicken

MAKES 4 SERVINGS

½ teaspoon salt
½ teaspoon onion powder
½ teaspoon granulated
  garlic
½ teaspoon celery seed
½ teaspoon dried basil
  leaves, crushed
½ teaspoon paprika
4 chicken thighs, skin and
  fat removed

4 chicken backs, skin and
  fat removed
2 tablespoons honey
2 tablespoons balsamic
  vinegar
2 tablespoons bottled chili
  sauce

Preheat the oven to 375°F.

Combine the first 6 ingredients in a small bowl. Mix well and sprinkle over the chicken. In a small bowl, combine the honey, vinegar and chili sauce and mix well. Spoon *half* of the mixture over the chicken. Refrigerate for 1 hour to marinate. Place the chicken in a baking dish that has been sprayed with nonstick vegetable cooking spray. Cover and bake for 20 minutes. Uncover and spoon the remaining mixture over the chicken. Increase the heat to 450°F and bake 20 minutes longer.

PER SERVING	KCAL	FATgm	CHOLmg	SODmg
	209	8.3	98	343

Chicken in Red Wine Sauce

In the restaurant, this seems to be everyone's favorite dish!

MAKES 4 SERVINGS

½ teaspoon salt
½ teaspoon garlic powder
½ teaspoon chili powder
¼ teaspoon ground red
    pepper
4 chicken thighs, skin and
    fat removed
3 tablespoons all-purpose
    flour
½ cup chopped onions

¼ cup chopped green bell
    pepper
¼ cup chopped red bell
    pepper
1 cup salt-free chicken
    broth
½ cup red wine
¼ cup plain nonfat yogurt
2 cups hot cooked rice

Preheat the oven to 450°F.

Sprinkle the salt, garlic powder, chili powder and red pepper over the chicken. Spray the inside of a medium skillet with non-stick vegetable cooking spray and place over high heat. Add the chicken and sauté for 10 minutes, or until browned on all sides, turning often. Stir in the flour and cook for 1 minute, stirring constantly. Add the onions and bell peppers; cook and stir for 5 minutes. Stir in the broth and wine and cook 15 minutes. Stir in the yogurt, reduce the heat to medium and cook 15 minutes longer, stirring often.

Place the chicken in a 9-inch-square baking dish. Spoon the sauce over the chicken and bake, uncovered, for 20 minutes. Serve the chicken over the rice.

PER SERVING	KCAL	FATgm	CHOLmg	SODmg
	145	5.9	49	307

Chicken Divine

The smooth and delicate sauce in this recipe comes from the blended vegetables. Try it, it really is divine!

MAKES 6 SERVINGS

One 2½-to-3-pound
　chicken, skinned and
　cut into serving pieces
1 large carrot, diced (about
　1 cup)
1 cup chopped onions
¼ cup chopped green bell
　pepper
¼ cup chopped celery
½ teaspoon salt

½ teaspoon paprika
¼ teaspoon ground white
　pepper
2 cups water
2 tablespoons chopped fresh
　parsley
One 10¾-ounce can 99%
　fat-free condensed
　cream of mushroom
　soup

Spray the inside of a 5-quart Dutch oven with butter-flavored nonstick vegetable cooking spray. Place over high heat until very hot. Add the chicken and sauté for 5 minutes, or until browned on all sides, turning often to prevent burning. Add the next 7 ingredients; cook, stirring, 10 minutes longer. Pour in *1½ cups* of the water; cover and cook an additional 10 minutes. Add the parsley and cook, covered, 5 minutes more.

Remove from the heat. Place the chicken on a platter and keep warm. Transfer the sautéed vegetables and liquid to a food processor and puree. Return the pureed vegetables to the same pot over high heat. Add the cream of mushroom soup and the remaining ½ cup water. Cook and stir for 2 minutes, then remove from the heat and spoon over the chicken.

PER SERVING	KCAL	FATgm	CHOLmg	SODmg
	342	13.2	156	323

Buttermilk Chicken

One 2½-pound chicken,   *1 cup Buttermilk Salad*
   skinned and cut into   *Dressing (page 30)*
   serving pieces   *2 cups corn flakes*

Place the chicken in a medium bowl and add the buttermilk mixture; mix well and refrigerate for 1 hour.

Meanwhile, preheat the oven to 350°F.

Place the corn flakes in a food processor and, using the pulse button, pulse 2 or 3 times, until coarsely crumbled. Drain the chicken, then dredge in the corn flakes. Spray a baking sheet with nonstick vegetable cooking spray. Arrange the chicken pieces on the baking sheet about 1 inch apart. Bake about 35 minutes, or until the chicken is tender.

PER SERVING	KCAL	FATgm	CHOLmg	SODmg
	353	13.2	155	252

Chicken Cacciatore

A *classic Italian favorite. Serve over rice or pasta.*

MAKES 6 SERVINGS

*1 teaspoon dried basil
leaves, crushed*
½ teaspoon salt
*½ teaspoon ground white
pepper*
*½ teaspoon ground red
pepper*
*One 2½-pound chicken, cut
into serving pieces*
2 cups chopped onions

*1 cup thinly sliced fresh
mushrooms*
2 tablespoons tomato paste
*1 cup salt-free chicken
broth*
*5 plum tomatoes, peeled,
seeded and chopped*
*¼ cup finely chopped green
onions*

Combine the basil, salt, white pepper and red pepper and sprinkle over both sides of the chicken. Spray the inside of a large skillet with butter-flavored nonstick vegetable cooking spray and place over high heat. Add the chicken and sauté for 10 minutes, or until it is browned on all sides. Add the onions and mushrooms and cook 5 minutes longer, stirring often. Dissolve the tomato paste in the broth and add to the skillet along with the tomatoes. Cover and cook for 15 minutes, stirring well. Add the green onions and cook 5 minutes longer, stirring often.

PER SERVING	KCAL	FATgm	CHOLmg	SODmg
	294	9.7	129	289

Chili Chicken

MAKES 4 SERVINGS

1 tablespoon chili powder
½ teaspoon salt
*½ teaspoon granulated
 garlic*
½ teaspoon ground oregano

½ teaspoon paprika
*One 2½-to-3-pound
 chicken, skin and fat
 removed*

Preheat the oven to 375°F.

In a small bowl, combine all the seasonings; mix well and sprinkle over the chicken and inside the cavity. Spray the inside of a 9-by-5-inch loaf pan with nonstick vegetable cooking spray. Place the chicken in the pan, cover with aluminum foil and bake for 30 minutes. Remove from the oven and spray the chicken with vegetable cooking spray. Baste with pan juices, cover and bake 30 minutes longer, or until the chicken is done.

PER SERVING	KCAL	FATgm	CHOLmg	SODmg
	271	9.8	129	383

99

Chimi-Chimi Chicken

MAKES 3 SERVINGS

FOR THE CHICKEN FILLING

½ pound skinned and boned chicken breast, cut into 1-inch strips
3 thin strips yellow bell pepper
3 thin strips green bell pepper
3 thin strips red bell pepper
1 teaspoon onion powder
⅛ teaspoon salt
⅛ teaspoon ground marjoram
1 cup water

FOR THE TOMATO-CHILI SAUCE

½ cup low-sodium tomato sauce
¼ cup water

1 tablespoon low-sodium Worcestershire sauce
1 tablespoon salt-free chicken bouillon granules
1 teaspoon chili powder
½ teaspoon dried basil leaves, crushed

FOR THE CHEESE TOPPING

1 cup low-fat cottage cheese
3 tablespoons chopped black olives
3 tablespoons chopped onion

Three 8-inch flour tortillas

TO PREPARE CHICKEN FILLING: Spray the inside of a medium skillet with nonstick vegetable cooking spray and place over high heat. Add the chicken and sauté for 5 minutes. Add the bell peppers, onion powder, salt and marjoram and continue cooking for 3 minutes, stirring often. Reduce the heat to a simmer, add the water and cook an additional 3 minutes. Remove from heat; set aside and keep warm.

TO PREPARE TOMATO-CHILI SAUCE: In a small saucepan over medium heat, combine all the sauce ingredients. Cook for 8 minutes, or until the sauce thickens, stirring often. Set aside and keep warm.

TO PREPARE CHEESE TOPPING: Place the cottage cheese in a blender and process till smooth. Stir in the olives and onion; set aside.

TO PREPARE TORTILLAS: Spray the inside of a medium skillet with nonstick vegetable cooking spray. Place over high heat and brown the tortillas one at a time, about 1 minute per side.

TO ASSEMBLE: Preheat the oven to 350°F. Spray an 8-inch-square baking dish with nonstick vegetable cooking spray and set aside. Spoon one-third of the chicken filling across the center of each tortilla. Roll up the tortillas and place seam side down in the baking dish. Top with the tomato-chili sauce and bake for 10 minutes. Spoon the cheese topping across the tortillas and serve hot.

PER SERVING	KCAL	FATgm	CHOLmg	SODmg
	305	5.7	68	492

South of the Border Chicken

MAKES 6 SERVINGS

Six 8-inch flour tortillas,
  quartered
4 cups water
One 2½-pound chicken,
  skin and fat removed
2 jalapeño peppers, thinly
  sliced
1 cup thinly sliced fresh
  mushrooms
½ cup finely chopped
  onions
¼ cup finely chopped red
  bell pepper
½ teaspoon granulated
  garlic

½ teaspoon dried basil
  leaves, crushed
¼ teaspoon salt
¼ teaspoon dried oregano
  leaves, crushed
One 10-ounce can reduced-
  calorie cream of
  mushroom soup
1½ cups salt-free chicken
  broth
½ cup evaporated skim
  milk
Three ¾-ounce slices
  reduced-fat American
  cheese product

Preheat the oven to 375°F.

Arrange tortillas on a baking sheet that has been sprayed with nonstick vegetable cooking spray. Bake for 15 minutes, or until crisp; remove from the oven and set aside. In a 5-quart Dutch oven over high heat, bring the water to a boil. Add the chicken; reduce the heat to medium and cook, covered, for 20 minutes, or until the chicken is tender. Remove the chicken and let cool to the touch, then debone and cube the meat; set aside.

Spray the inside of a medium skillet with nonstick vegetable cooking spray and place over high heat. Add the next 8 ingredients and sauté for 5 minutes. Stir in the mushroom soup, broth, milk and cooked chicken; cook and stir for 5 minutes. Add the cheese and continue cooking until it is melted. Remove from the heat and set aside. Place a layer of tortillas in a 9-inch-square baking dish that has been sprayed with nonstick vegetable cooking spray. Spoon in the meat mixture, then top with the remaining tortillas. Bake for 30 minutes.

PER SERVING	KCAL	FATgm	CHOLmg	SODmg
	319	9.9	87	662

Chicken Enchiladas

*T*his dish is very spicy; use half of the pepper for a less spicy flavor.

MAKES 6 SERVINGS

6 cups water
One 2½-pound chicken,
  skin and fat removed
2 cups finely chopped
  onions
3 dried hot chili peppers,
  crushed
2 tablespoons sliced
  jalapeño pepper
¼ teaspoon ground cumin
¼ teaspoon ground oregano

2 tablespoons tomato paste
One 12-ounce can
  evaporated skim milk
½ cup shredded reduced-fat
  Cheddar-Jack cheese
3 tablespoons reduced-fat
  ricotta cheese
Six 8-inch flour tortillas
⅓ cup shredded part-skim
  mozzarella cheese

Preheat the oven to 375°F.

In a large stockpot over high heat, bring the water to a boil. Add the chicken and cook for 20 minutes, or until it is tender. Remove from the heat; lift out the chicken and reserve 2½ cups of the stock. Let the chicken cool to the touch, then debone, shred and set aside.

Spray the inside of a medium skillet with nonstick vegetable cooking spray and place over high heat. Add the onions and sauté for 5 minutes. Add the dried chili peppers, jalapeño, cumin, oregano and salt; cook and stir for 3 minutes. Dissolve the tomato paste in the reserved stock and add to the skillet; cook, stirring, for 15 minutes. Add the milk and cook 10 minutes longer, stirring often. Add the Cheddar-Jack, ricotta and chicken. Remove from the heat and stir until the cheese is melted; set aside.

In a small cast-iron skillet over medium heat, brown the tortillas for 1 minute on each side. Spoon equal portions of the chicken mixture into the middle of each tortilla. Fold the tortillas in thirds and place seam side down in a 9-inch-square baking dish that has been sprayed with nonstick vegetable cooking spray. Spoon the remaining chicken mixture over the tortillas and top with the mozzarella cheese. Bake for 10 minutes.

PER SERVING	KCAL	FATgm	CHOLmg	SODmg
	441	12.3	132	370

Three-Pepper Chicken Enchiladas

My teenage granddaughter made this dish for a slumber party. All the kids enjoyed making their own enchiladas.

MAKES 8 SERVINGS

1 cup low-fat cottage cheese
1 tablespoon lemon juice
2 teaspoons salt-free lemon-pepper seasoning
½ teaspoon salt
1 pound skinned and boned chicken breast, cut into ⅛-inch strips
½ yellow bell pepper, thinly sliced

½ red bell pepper, thinly sliced
½ green bell pepper, thinly sliced
One-half 6-ounce can salt-free tomato juice
Eight 8-inch flour tortillas
One 4-ounce can sliced jalapēno peppers, drained (optional)
1 cup shredded lettuce
2 medium tomatoes, peeled, seeded and chopped (about 1 cup)

Place the cottage cheese and lemon juice in a blender and process until smooth; set aside. Sprinkle the lemon-pepper seasoning and salt over the chicken. Spray the inside of a large skillet with nonstick vegetable cooking spray and place over high heat. Add the chicken and bell peppers and sauté for 10 minutes. Add the tomato juice and cook 5 minutes longer.

In a small cast-iron skillet over medium heat, brown the tortillas for 1 minute on each side. Place the tortillas on serving plates and put equal portions of chicken mixture, chili peppers, lettuce and tomatoes in the center of each. Fold the tortillas into thirds and place seam side down. Spoon *1 tablespoon* of the blended cottage cheese on top of each tortilla if desired.

PER SERVING	KCAL	FATgm	CHOLmg	SODmg
	205	**4**	**48**	**168**

Curried Chicken

After my accountant, Essie LeBlanc, had a heart attack, he had to change his eating habits. His wife, Beverly, cooks many recipes from my first book for him, but she wanted something new. When I created this dish, I let him be my taste tester. It is now one of their favorite dishes.

MAKES 5 SERVINGS

½ teaspoon salt
½ teaspoon granulated
    garlic
½ teaspoon ground white
    pepper
¼ teaspoon curry powder
1 pound skinned and boned
    chicken breast halves
2 cups thinly sliced fresh
    mushrooms
½ cup finely chopped
    onions

⅓ cup finely chopped red
    bell pepper
½ cup salt-free chicken
    broth
½ teaspoon cornstarch
½ cup white wine
2 tablespoons water
⅛ teaspoon browning and
    seasoning sauce

Combine the first 4 ingredients in a small bowl and mix well. Sprinkle over both sides of the chicken; set aside. Spray the inside of a medium skillet with nonstick vegetable cooking spray and place over high heat. Add the chicken breasts and sauté for 5 minutes, turning often to prevent burning. Add the mushrooms,

onions and bell pepper; cook and stir for 5 minutes, scraping the skillet with a wooden spoon.

Slowly add the broth and cook for 10 minutes, stirring often. Mix the remaining ingredients together, then pour into the skillet. Cook and stir 15 minutes longer.

PER SERVING	KCAL	FATgm	CHOLmg	SODmg
	184	3.5	77	278

Chicken with Apricots

MAKES 4 SERVINGS

½ cup dried apricots
One 8-ounce can apricot
  juice
2 tablespoons apricot
  preserves
1 teaspoon cornstarch
2 tablespoons water

1 teaspoon salt
1 teaspoon granulated
  garlic
¼ teaspoon ground red
  pepper
One 3-pound chicken, skin
  and fat removed

Preheat the oven to 375°F.

In a small saucepan over high heat, combine the apricots, juice and preserves and bring to boil. Cook for 10 minutes, stirring often. Reduce the heat to medium. Dissolve the cornstarch in the water and add to the saucepan. Cook and stir 10 minutes longer. Remove from the heat and set aside.

Combine the salt, garlic and red pepper and sprinkle over the chicken and inside the cavity. Place in a baking dish and bake for 30 minutes, basting often with the apricot sauce.

PER SERVING	KCAL	FATgm	CHOLmg	SODmg
	325	9.5	129	611

Chicken with Sweet Potatoes

*T*he natural sweetness from the sweet potatoes gives this chicken dish a flavor all its own!

MAKES 6 SERVINGS

2 cups water
1 sweet potato, peeled and
    sliced ½ inch thick
½ teaspoon dried oregano
    leaves, crushed
¼ teaspoon salt
One 2½-pound chicken,
    skinned and halved

¼ cup brown sugar
1 teaspoon cornstarch
¼ teaspoon ground
    cinnamon
½ cup hot salt-free chicken
    broth

Preheat the oven to 400°F.

In a medium saucepan, bring the water to a boil over high heat. Add the potato slices and cook for 10 minutes, or until crisp-tender. Drain and set aside. Sprinkle the oregano and salt over the chicken. Place the chicken in a 11-by-9-inch baking dish that has been sprayed with nonstick vegetable cooking spray. Arrange the potato slices around the chicken. Dissolve the brown sugar, cornstarch and cinnamon in the hot broth; pour over the chicken. Cover with aluminum foil and bake for 30 minutes. Uncover and bake 30 minutes longer, or until the chicken is brown, basting several times.

PER SERVING	KCAL	FATgm	CHOLmg	SODmg
	220	6.8	87	166

Chicken and Dumplings

MAKES 4 SERVINGS

FOR THE DUMPLINGS
1/2 cup all-purpose flour
1/2 teaspoon baking powder
1/4 teaspoon salt
1/4 teaspoon ground red
　pepper
1/4 cup evaporated skim
　milk
2 tablespoons egg
　substitute
2 tablespoons very finely
　chopped fresh parsley

FOR THE CHICKEN
1/2 teaspoon paprika
1/2 teaspoon ground black
　pepper

1/4 teaspoon salt
1 pound skinned and boned
　chicken breast halves
1 cup finely chopped onions
1/2 cup finely chopped celery
1/2 cup finely chopped green
　bell pepper
1/2 cup salt-free chicken
　broth
1 cup evaporated skim milk

To Prepare the Dumplings: In a small bowl, combine the flour, baking powder, salt and red pepper; mix well. Stir in the milk, egg substitute and parsley, stirring well; set aside.

To Prepare the Chicken: Sprinkle the paprika, black pepper and salt over both sides of the chicken. Spray the inside of a large skillet with nonstick vegetable cooking spray and place over high heat. Add the chicken and sauté for 15 minutes, turning often to

prevent burning. Add the onions, celery and bell pepper; cook and stir for 10 minutes. Stir in the broth and cook for 5 minutes. Stir in the milk; reduce the heat to medium and drop the dumpling dough, 1 teaspoon at a time, into the skillet. Cook the dough for 2 minutes on each side. Reduce the heat to a simmer and cook 5 minutes longer.

PER SERVING	KCAL	FATgm	CHOLmg	SODmg
	313	4.6	99	478

Baked Chicken with Fruit Chutney

The fruit chutney I created to go with this dish tastes so delicious, my taste testers insisted that I use it on other dishes as well.

MAKES 4 SERVINGS

½ teaspoon salt
½ teaspoon paprika
¼ teaspoon granulated garlic
¼ teaspoon onion powder
¼ teaspoon ground red pepper

⅛ teaspoon ground cinnamon
⅛ teaspoon ground nutmeg
4 chicken thighs, skinned

Preheat the oven to 500°F.

Combine all the dry seasonings in a small bowl. Mix well and sprinkle over both sides of the chicken. Arrange the chicken in a 9-inch-square baking dish that has been sprayed with nonstick vegetable cooking spray. Cover and bake for 20 minutes. Uncover and bake 20 minutes longer. Remove from oven and transfer to a platter. Top with Fruit Chutney (page 305).

PER SERVING	KCAL	FATgm	CHOLmg	SODmg
	112	5.8	49	291

Blue Cheese Chicken

1 teaspoon granulated
  garlic
½ teaspoon salt
½ teaspoon paprika
½ teaspoon ground red
  pepper
½ teaspoon ground black
  pepper

One 2½-pound chicken
1 tablespoon browning and
  seasoning sauce
1 cup bottled fat-free blue
  cheese dressing
1 large onion, quartered
1 cup water
½ cup chopped red bell
  pepper

Preheat the oven to 375°F.

Sprinkle the garlic, salt, paprika, red pepper and black pepper over the chicken and inside the cavity. Using a pastry brush, brush the browning and seasoning sauce and *half* of the blue cheese dressing over the chicken; reserve the remaining dressing. Put the onion inside the cavity of the chicken. Place the chicken in a 9-inch-square baking dish that has been sprayed with butter-flavored nonstick vegetable cooking spray. Add the water to the dish, cover and bake for 20 minutes. Uncover and bake 20 minutes longer, basting with pan juices several times while cooking. Remove from the oven and reserve the pan juices. Remove the onion from the chicken cavity and set aside. Let the chicken cool to the touch; cut into quarters, place on a platter and keep warm.

In a medium skillet over high heat, combine the bell pepper, reserved onion and reserved pan juices. Cook and stir for 10 minutes. Remove from the heat, transfer to a blender and puree. Return to the same skillet over medium heat. Add the remaining blue cheese dressing and cook 3 minutes longer, stirring often. Remove from the heat and spoon the sauce over the chicken.

PER SERVING	KCAL	FATgm	CHOLmg	SODmg
	316	9.5	129	604

Stuffed Cornish Hens

MAKES 6 SERVINGS

1 tablespoon salt-free
   lemon-pepper
   seasoning
1 teaspoon salt
1 teaspoon chili powder
1 teaspoon ground red
   pepper
½ teaspoon paprika
Two 1-pound Cornish game
   hens
½ pound ground turkey
   breast

1 cup chopped onions
½ cup chopped green bell
   pepper
½ cup chopped red bell
   pepper
One-half 10-ounce can 99%
   fat-free condensed
   cream of chicken soup
1 cup cooked rice

Preheat the oven to 450°F.

In a small bowl, combine the first 5 ingredients; mix well and reserve 1 tablespoon for later use. Sprinkle the remaining seasoning mix over the hens; set aside.

Spray the inside of a large skillet with butter-flavored nonstick vegetable cooking spray and place over high heat. Add the turkey and sauté for 5 minutes. Add the onions, bell peppers and the reserved seasoning mix. Cook and stir for 5 minutes. Add the soup and rice; mix well. Remove from the heat; reserve 1½ cups of the rice mixture and set aside, keeping warm.

Spoon equal amounts of the remaining rice mixture into the cavity of each hen, then secure the legs with cooking string. Cover and bake for 25 minutes, or until the hens are tender. Remove from the oven; cut the string and discard. Place the reserved rice mixture on a platter and place the hens over the rice.

PER SERVING	KCAL	FATgm	CHOLmg	SODmg
	192	3.7	75	392

Old-fashioned Pot-Roasted Hen

MAKES 2 SERVINGS

1 tablespoon salt-free
    chicken bouillon
    granules
1½ cups water
½ teaspoon salt
½ teaspoon sugar (optional)
½ teaspoon granulated
    garlic
½ teaspoon onion powder
½ teaspoon Spanish
    paprika
½ teaspoon ground black
    pepper

One 1½-to-2-pound Cornish
    game hen, skin and fat
    removed
6 pearl onions, peeled
1 small carrot, thinly sliced
½ pound small new
    potatoes
½ cup chopped celery
4 plum tomatoes, peeled,
    seeded and chopped

Dissolve the bouillon granules in the water and set aside. Combine the salt, sugar, garlic, onion powder, paprika and black pepper in a small bowl. Mix well and sprinkle *half* of the seasoning mix over the hen and inside the cavity; reserve the remaining seasoning.

Spray the inside of a 5-quart Dutch oven with nonstick vegetable cooking spray and place over medium heat. Add the hen and sauté for 20 minutes, or until browned on all sides, turning often. Add the onions, carrot, potatoes, celery and ½ *cup* of the dissolved bouillon. Cover and cook for 15 minutes, stirring often. Add the tomatoes, reserved seasoning mix and remaining dissolved bouillon. Cook, covered, 15 minutes longer or until the hen and vegetables are tender.

PER SERVING	KCAL	FATgm	CHOLmg	SODmg
	447	10.2	129	678

Oven-Barbecued Hen

The great barbecue flavor of this dish makes it taste like it was just cooked outdoors.

MAKES 4 SERVINGS

1 teaspoon onion powder
1 teaspoon garlic powder
¼ teaspoon dried basil
    leaves, crushed
One 1½-pound Cornish
    game hen, quartered,
    skin and fat removed

½ cup salt-free catsup
1 tablespoon low-sodium
    soy sauce
1 tablespoon lemon juice
½ teaspoon hot pepper
    sauce

Preheat the oven to 375°F.

Sprinkle the onion powder, garlic powder and basil over the hen. In a small bowl, combine the catsup, soy sauce, lemon juice and hot sauce; mix well. Place the hen in a 9-inch-square baking dish. Spoon *half* of the catsup mixture over the hen; cover and bake for 20 minutes.

Increase the temperature to 450°F. Uncover the hen, baste with the remaining sauce, and bake 15 minutes longer. To brown, place the hen under the broiler 6 inches from heat for 3 minutes, or until golden brown.

PER SERVING	KCAL	FATgm	CHOLmg	SODmg
	302	6	144	465

Baked Turkey Breasts

This dish can be prepared ahead of time. Cover and refriger-ate until ready to cook.

MAKES 8 SERVINGS

1 teaspoon salt
½ teaspoon ground white
    pepper
2 pounds turkey breast
    cutlets
1 small onion, peeled and
    quartered

1 small zucchini or yellow
    squash, thinly sliced
½ small green bell pepper,
    cut into ½-inch cubes
½ small red bell pepper, cut
    into ½-inch cubes
¼ cup water

Preheat the oven to 350°F.

Sprinkle the salt and pepper over both sides of the meat; place in an 8-inch-square baking dish. Arrange the onion, squash and bell peppers around the meat. Pour in the water, cover and bake for 1 hour.

PER SERVING	KCAL	FATgm	CHOLmg	SODmg
	220	1.3	126	413

Turkey-Vegetable Stir-fry

MAKES 4 SERVINGS

1 pound boneless turkey
    breast, cut into thin
    strips
1 small onion, thinly sliced
1 small zucchini, thinly
    sliced
½ green bell pepper, thinly
    sliced
½ red bell pepper, thinly
    sliced
2 tablespoons low-sodium
    Worcestershire sauce

¼ teaspoon salt
¼ teaspoon ground white
    pepper
¼ teaspoon dried hot chili
    pepper
2 teaspoons cornstarch
1 cup salt-free chicken
    broth
One 15-ounce can whole
    baby corn, drained

Spray the inside of a large skillet with nonstick vegetable cooking spray and place over high heat. Add the turkey and sauté for 5 minutes. Add the onion, zucchini and bell peppers; cook and stir for 5 minutes. Add the next 4 ingredients and cook, stirring, for 10 minutes. Dissolve the cornstarch in the broth and add to the skillet along with the baby corn. Cook and stir 5 minutes longer, or until the turkey is tender.

PER SERVING	KCAL	FATgm	CHOLmg	SODmg
	236	1.4	95	228

Honey-Mustard Turkey

The blend of natural honey with the slight tang of mustard gives this turkey dish a taste that's not for the birds!

MAKES 2 SERVINGS

1 teaspoon cornstarch
½ cup water
½ pound thinly sliced
    turkey breast cutlets
1 cup finely chopped onions
¼ teaspoon salt
¼ teaspoon ground red
    pepper

2 tablespoons honey
2 tablespoons Dijon
    mustard
1 teaspoon grated fresh
    ginger

Dissolve the cornstarch in the water and set aside. Spray the inside of a medium skillet with nonstick vegetable cooking spray and place over high heat. Add the turkey and sauté for 10 minutes, or until browned, turning often. Add the onions, salt and red pepper; cook and stir for 5 minutes. Add the dissolved cornstarch, honey and mustard. Reduce the heat to medium and cook for 5 minutes. Add the ginger; cook 10 minutes longer, or until the turkey is tender, stirring often.

PER SERVING	KCAL	FATgm	CHOLmg	SODmg
	268	2.1	95	513

Turkey Lafayette

MAKES 3 SERVINGS

¼ teaspoon salt
¼ teaspoon ground thyme
¼ teaspoon ground red
    pepper
½ pound skinned and
    boned turkey breast,
    sliced in half
    lengthwise
1 cup finely chopped onions
½ cup finely chopped green
    bell pepper
½ cup finely chopped red
    bell pepper

2 ounces Smoked Turkey
    Sausage (page 144)
    finely chopped
1 tablespoon salt-free
    chicken bouillon
    granules
1 cup water
2 slices bread (40 calories
    per slice), made into
    crumbs

Preheat the oven to 350°F.

Sprinkle the salt, thyme and red pepper over the turkey and set aside. Spray the inside of a medium skillet with nonstick vegetable cooking spray and place over high heat. Add the onions, bell peppers and sausage; sauté for 10 minutes. Dissolve the bouillon granules in the water and add to the skillet. Cook for 10 minutes, stirring often. Remove from the heat and stir in the bread crumbs; let cool to the touch.

Spoon the cooked mixture down the center of one breast half; top with the remaining breast half and tie with cooking string. Place in a baking dish that has been sprayed with nonstick vegetable cooking spray. Cover and bake for 20 minutes. Uncover and bake 5 minutes longer.

PER SERVING	KCAL	FATgm	CHOLmg	SODmg
	152	1.5	61	232

Turkey and Grits Grand Coteau

MAKES 4 SERVINGS

¾ cup uncooked white grits
1 pound ground turkey
   breast
½ teaspoon salt
½ teaspoon dried basil
   leaves, crushed
¼ teaspoon ground oregano
One 14-ounce can salt-free
   whole tomatoes
One 4-ounce can chopped
   hot green chili peppers

2 fresh jalapeño peppers,
   minced (about ⅓ cup)
2 teaspoons granulated
   garlic
One 16-ounce can whole-
   kernel corn, drained
½ cup reduced-fat ricotta
   cheese
2 ounces reduced-calorie
   processed cheese
   spread, thinly sliced

Cook the grits according to package directions; set aside. Spray the inside of two 9-inch-square baking dishes with nonstick vegetable cooking spray. Spoon equal portions of the grits into each baking dish and refrigerate for 2 hours.

Spray the inside of a large skillet with nonstick vegetable cooking spray and place over high heat. Add the turkey, salt, basil and oregano and sauté for 10 minutes. Add the tomatoes, chili peppers, jalapeños and garlic; continue cooking and stirring for 15 minutes, chopping the tomatoes with a spoon while cooking. Remove from the heat and set aside.

Preheat the oven to 350°F. Remove the grits from the refrigerator and spoon *half* of the meat mixture into one dish, spreading evenly. Then layer with the corn. Using a spatula, carefully remove the grits from the second dish and place on top of the corn. Spread the ricotta and processed cheese on top of the grits, then layer with the remaining meat mixture. Cover with aluminum foil and bake for 45 minutes. Serve warm.

PER SERVING	KCAL	FATgm	CHOLmg	SODmg
	384	6.8	112	891

Turkey-Stuffed Mirliton

Known as vegetable pears or chayotes in some areas, mirlitons are delicious when stuffed. This low-fat dish tastes incredibly rich.

Makes 10 servings

8 cups water
5 mirlitons, cut in half
1 pound ground turkey
    breast
1 cup chopped onions
½ cup chopped green bell
    pepper
½ cup chopped red bell
    pepper

½ teaspoon salt
½ teaspoon ground red
    pepper
1½ cups salt-free chicken
    broth
1 cup corn flakes, crushed
¼ cup fine dry bread
    crumbs
Paprika

Preheat the oven to 375°F.

In a 5-quart Dutch oven over high heat, bring the water to a boil. Add the mirlitons and cook for 8 minutes, or until crisp-tender. Remove from the heat and place the mirlitons in ice water for 4 minutes to cool. Using a spoon, carefully scoop out center of each mirliton leaving a ¼-inch shell. Coarsely chop the pulp and set aside 1½ cups. (Use remaining pulp in another recipe.)

Spray the inside of a large skillet with nonstick vegetable cooking spray and place over high heat. Add the turkey and sauté for 10 minutes. Add the onions, bell peppers, salt and red pepper; cook, stirring, for 10 minutes. Add the broth and stir, scraping the bottom of the skillet well. Add the reserved mirliton pulp and cook for 5 minutes, stirring often. Remove from the heat, add the corn flakes and mix well.

Fill each mirliton shell with the mixture and place in a 9-inch-square baking dish that has been sprayed with nonstick vegetable cooking spray. Sprinkle with bread crumbs and paprika. Bake for 20 minutes, or until heated through and the crumbs start to brown.

PER SERVING	KCAL	FATgm	CHOLmg	SODmg
	83	0.5	38	139

Turkey Meatballs with Mushroom Gravy

Once you try this dish, it will become one of your favorites.

MAKES 4 SERVINGS

1 pound ground turkey
    breast
2 slices bread (40 calories
    per slice), made into
    crumbs
1 teaspoon garlic powder
½ teaspoon salt
½ teaspoon ground red
    pepper
1 cup finely chopped onions
½ cup finely chopped green
    bell pepper
2 teaspoons salt-free
    chicken bouillon
    granules

1 cup water
1 cup thinly sliced fresh
    mushrooms
¼ cup finely chopped red
    bell pepper
½ cup evaporated skim
    milk
3 tablespoons reduced-
    calorie soft-style cream
    cheese
2 cups cooked bow-tie pasta

In a medium bowl, combine the meat, bread crumbs, garlic powder, salt and red pepper; mix well and shape into 16 small meatballs. Spray the inside of a large skillet with butter-flavored nonstick vegetable cooking spray and place over high heat. Add the meatballs; cover and cook for 10 minutes, shaking the skillet while cooking to prevent burning. Remove the meatballs and keep warm.

Spray the same skillet again with the cooking spray and place over high heat. Add the onions and green bell pepper and sauté for 5 minutes. Dissolve the bouillon granules in the water. Pour *half* of the dissolved bouillon into the skillet and cook for 10 minutes, stirring often. Add the remaining bouillon, the milk and cream cheese; cook and stir for 10 minutes. Remove from the heat and stir in the cooked pasta. Serve immediately.

PER SERVING	KCAL	FATgm	CHOLmg	SODmg
	237	2.4	96	384

Turkey Meatballs and Spaghetti

This is a great main dish. The kids will love it and it's a good way to introduce ground turkey to the whole family.

MAKES 6 SERVINGS

1 pound ground turkey breast
¼ cup finely chopped onion
½ teaspoon salt
¼ teaspoon ground white pepper
¼ teaspoon ground red pepper
1½ cups salt-free chicken broth
One 16-ounce can salt-free whole tomatoes

2 cups chopped onions
½ cup chopped green bell pepper
½ cup chopped celery
3 tablespoons tomato paste
1 teaspoon brown sugar
1 teaspoon dried basil leaves, crushed
½ teaspoon salt
½ teaspoon ground white pepper

Combine the first 5 ingredients in a medium bowl. Mix well and shape into 16 small meatballs. Spray the inside of a large skillet with nonstick vegetable cooking spray and place over high heat. Add the meatballs and sauté for 5 minutes, or until browned on all sides. Remove from the heat and set the meatballs aside. Pour ½ cup of the broth into the skillet to deglaze; reserve the liquid.

Spray the inside of a 5-quart Dutch oven with nonstick vegetable cooking spray and place over high heat. Add the reserved liquid and all the remaining ingredients. Cover and cook for 20 minutes. Add the meatballs and cook, covered, 15 minutes longer, stirring often.

PER SERVING	KCAL	FATgm	CHOLmg	SODmg
	158	1.3	63	380

Turkey Kabobs

MAKES 5 SERVINGS

1 pound skinned and boned
　turkey breast, cut into
　2-inch cubes
1 small onion, quartered
1 medium tomato,
　quartered
1 small green bell pepper,
　cut into 2-inch squares
1 small red bell pepper, cut
　into 2-inch squares

1 cup fat-free Italian
　dressing
1 tablespoon salt-free
　lemon-pepper
　seasoning
1/2 teaspoon dried oregano
　leaves, crushed
1/2 teaspoon ground red
　pepper
1/4 teaspoon salt

Place the turkey, onion, tomato and bell peppers in a plastic bag.
In a small bowl, combine the dressing, lemon-pepper seasoning,
oregano, red pepper and salt and mix well. Pour into the plastic
bag, seal and shake well. Refrigerate for 1 hour.

Meanwhile, preheat a charcoal or gas grill. Soak 5 wooden
skewers in cold water (this will keep them from burning). Arrange
the marinated turkey and vegetables on the skewers, then spray
with vegetable cooking spray. Place the skewers on the hot grill,
and cook for 20 minutes, turning often and brushing with the remaining marinade, until the meat is tender.

PER SERVING	KCAL	FATgm	CHOLmg	SODmg
	146	1	76	149

129

Italian Turkey with Mushrooms

A *great dish the whole family is sure to enjoy.*

MAKES 4 SERVINGS

2 teaspoons olive oil
2 cloves garlic
1 pound skinned and boned
    turkey breast, cut into
    1-inch strips
4 plum tomatoes, peeled,
    seeded and chopped
1 small zucchini, cut into
    julienne strips
½ large green bell pepper,
    cut into julienne strips
½ large red bell pepper, cut
    into julienne strips
1 cup thinly sliced fresh
    mushrooms
1 teaspoon dried Italian
    herbs

¾ teaspoon salt
½ teaspoon dried oregano
    leaves, crushed
½ teaspoon dried basil
    leaves, crushed
½ teaspoon ground red
    pepper
1 cup salt-free chicken
    broth
2 cups cooked fettuccine
3 tablespoons very finely
    chopped fresh parsley
2 tablespoons grated
    Parmesan cheese

In a large skillet over high heat, heat the oil. Add the garlic and
sauté for 1 minute, or until browned. Remove the garlic and discard. Add the meat and cook for 10 minutes, stirring often. Add
the tomatoes, zucchini, bell peppers and mushrooms; cook, stirring, for 2 to 3 minutes. Add the dried Italian herbs, *½ teaspoon*
of the salt, the oregano, basil and red pepper. Cook and stir for
10 minutes. Remove from the heat; transfer to a plate and keep
warm.

To the same skillet over high heat, add the broth and remaining salt and bring to a boil. When the liquid is reduced by half, add the meat and onion mixture and the cooked fettuccine; cook for 3 minutes, shaking the skillet a few times to prevent sticking. Remove from the heat; place on a warm platter and top with the parsley and cheese.

PER SERVING	KCAL	FATgm	CHOLmg	SODmg
	157	2.2	0	380

Turkey Meat Loaf

MAKES 4 SERVINGS

*1 pound ground turkey
   breast
2 slices bread (40 calories
   per slice), toasted and
   finely crumbled
1 tablespoon low-sodium
   soy sauce*

*1 tablespoon dehydrated
   onion
1 teaspoon salt
½ teaspoon celery seed
¼ teaspoon dried basil
   leaves, crushed*

Preheat the oven to 375°F.

Combine all the ingredients in a large bowl and mix well. Shape the mixture into a loaf and place in a loaf pan that has been sprayed with nonstick vegetable cooking spray. Bake for 30 minutes.

PER SERVING	KCAL	FATgm	CHOLmg	SODmg
	176	0.9	95	771

Texas Chili

While visiting friends in Texas, I was amazed at how many versions of chili Texans have. Here is my low-fat recipe.

MAKES 5 SERVINGS

3 tablespoons tomato paste
2 cups water
1½ pounds ground turkey
    breast
1 cup finely chopped onions
One 16-ounce can whole
    tomatoes, chopped
2 fresh jalapeño peppers,
    finely chopped
2 tablespoons chopped
    dried hot chili peppers
2 tablespoons chili powder

2 teaspoons granulated
    garlic
1 teaspoon salt
1 teaspoon ground cumin
One 15-ounce can chili
    beans, rinsed and
    drained
½ cup shredded reduced-fat
    Cheddar cheese
    (optional)

Dissolve the tomato paste in the water and set aside. Spray the inside of a 5-quart Dutch oven with butter-flavored nonstick vegetable cooking spray and place over high heat. Add the ground turkey and onions and sauté for 10 minutes, or until the turkey is browned. Add the dissolved tomato paste and chopped tomatoes; cook, stirring, for 5 minutes.

Add the next 6 ingredients; cook and stir for 10 minutes. Add the beans and cook 10 minutes longer. Top each bowl of chili with *1 tablespoon* of the cheese if desired.

PER SERVING	KCAL	FATgm	CHOLmg	SODmg
	321	2.9	115	658

Turkey Burritos

The canned chili peppers used in this recipe have color-coded labels. The green is for mild, the orange is medium and the red is hot. I use mild, but use the one that's right for your taste buds!

Eight 6-inch flour tortillas
1 pound ground turkey breast
½ cup finely chopped onions
½ teaspoon salt
½ teaspoon ground white pepper
½ teaspoon ground red pepper
One 4-ounce can chopped green chili peppers

1 cup shredded iceberg lettuce
1 large tomato, peeled, seeded and chopped (about 1 cup)
1 ounce shredded reduced-fat Cheddar cheese
Guacamole Sauce (page 285)

In a small iron skillet over medium heat, brown the tortillas for 1 minute on each side. Place tortillas in aluminum foil and keep warm.

Spray the inside of a medium skillet with nonstick vegetable cooking spray and place over high heat. Add the ground turkey, onions, salt, white pepper and red pepper; sauté for 5 minutes,

or until the turkey is browned. Add the chili peppers; cook and stir 2 minutes longer, or until the onions are crisp-tender.

Place the tortillas on 8 serving plates and spoon equal portions of the turkey mixture into the middle of each; top with equal portions of the lettuce, tomatoes and cheese and 1 tablespoon of the guacamole sauce. Fold each tortilla in half and serve.

PER SERVING	KCAL	FATgm	CHOLmg	SODmg
	411	7.6	100	399

Mexican Turkey Pie

FOR THE FILLING

1 pound ground turkey
    breast
1 cup finely chopped onions
1/2 cup finely chopped green
    bell pepper
2 dried hot chili peppers,
    crushed
2 tablespoons chili powder
1/2 teaspoon salt
1/4 teaspoon dried oregano
    leaves, crushed
1/4 teaspoon ground cumin
2 tablespoons salt-free
    chicken bouillon
    granules

1 cup water
1/2 cup evaporated skim
    milk
1/4 cup finely chopped green
    onions
1/2 cup shredded reduced-fat
    Cheddar cheese

FOR THE DOUGH

2 cups masa harina
1 cup warm water
1/4 teaspoon salt

TO PREPARE THE FILLING: Spray the inside of a heavy skillet with vegetable cooking spray and place over high heat. Add the turkey and sauté for 8 minutes, or until browned. Add the onions, bell pepper, chili peppers, chili powder, salt, oregano and cumin; cook, stirring, for 10 minutes. Dissolve the bouillon granules in the water and add to skillet along with the milk. Cook and stir for 5 minutes. Remove from the heat and stir in the green onions; set aside.

TO PREPARE THE DOUGH: Combine all the ingredients in a medium bowl; stir until the dough forms a ball.

To Assemble: Preheat the oven to 350°F. Spray the inside of a 9-inch-square baking dish with nonstick vegetable cooking spray. Divide the dough in half; roll out each half to a ¼-inch thickness. Put one half inside baking dish, pressing down with the fingers. Spoon in the meat filling and add the cheese. Top with the remaining dough. Bake for 20 minutes.

PER SERVING	KCAL	FATgm	CHOLmg	SODmg
	175	2.2	67	375

Turkey Enchiladas

1 pound ground turkey
 breast
¼ cup very finely chopped
 onion
1 tablespoon low-sodium
 Worcestershire sauce
½ teaspoon salt
1½ cups evaporated skim
 milk
One 4-ounce can mild
 chopped green chili
 peppers with liquid

1 ounce reduced-fat
 Velveeta cheese
1 teaspoon cornstarch
½ cup water
4 dried hot chili peppers,
 crushed
1 teaspoon dried oregano
 leaves, crushed
½ teaspoon ground cumin
4 flour tortillas
1 ounce shredded reduced-
 fat Cheddar cheese

Spray the inside of a large skillet with butter-flavored nonstick vegetable cooking spray and place over high heat. Add the turkey and sauté for 10 minutes, or until browned. Add the onion, Worcestershire sauce and salt; cook and stir for 5 minutes. Remove from the heat; transfer to a bowl and set aside. Spray the same skillet again with the cooking spray and place over high heat. Add *1 cup* of the milk, the canned chili peppers and the Velveeta, stirring well. Combine the meat and milk mixture to use for the filling, stir well and set aside.

 Dissolve the cornstarch in the water and add to the skillet along with the remaining ½ cup milk, dried chili peppers, oregano and cumin. Cook and stir for 5 minutes, or until the sauce thickens. Remove from the heat; set aside.

In a small cast-iron skillet over medium heat, brown the tortillas for 1 minute on each side. Spoon ¼ cup of the filling into the middle of each tortilla; fold the tortilla in thirds across the filling and turn it seam side down. Carefully place the tortillas in a 9-inch-square baking dish that has been sprayed with the cooking spray. Spoon the remaining sauce over the tortillas. Top with the Cheddar cheese and bake for 15 minutes, or until the cheese is melted.

PER SERVING	KCAL	FATgm	CHOLmg	SODmg
	283	3.4	107	597

Mexican Goulash

Traditionally, goulash is made with ground beef, but I use ground turkey and low-fat cheese in this recipe. The end result is outstanding—and low in fat!

MAKES SIX 1-CUP SERVINGS

1 pound ground turkey breast
½ cup finely chopped onions
½ cup finely chopped green bell pepper
½ cup finely chopped red bell pepper
3 small dried hot chilies, crushed
1 teaspoon salt
½ teaspoon ground cumin
¼ cup tomato paste

1 cup water
One 10½-ounce can reduced-calorie cream of mushroom soup
½ cup white wine
2 cups cooked rotini (corkscrew-shaped pasta)
¼ cup shredded part-skim mozzarella cheese
½ cup fine dry bread crumbs

Preheat the oven to 375°F.

Spray the inside of a large skillet with nonstick vegetable cooking spray and place over high heat. Add the ground turkey and sauté for 10 minutes, or until browned. Add the onions and bell peppers and cook, stirring, for 10 minutes. Add the chilies, salt and cumin and cook 5 minutes longer. Dissolve the tomato paste in the water. Add to the skillet along with the mushroom soup

and wine; cook and stir for 10 minutes. Add the pasta and cheese and cook 1 minute more, stirring well.

Spoon the mixture into a 9-inch-square baking dish that has been sprayed with nonstick vegetable cooking spray. Sprinkle with the bread crumbs. Bake for 15 minutes, or until bubbling hot.

PER SERVING	KCAL	FATgm	CHOLmg	SODmg
	237	2.5	63	658

Turkey Fiesta

MAKES 5 SERVINGS

1 pound skinned and boned
    turkey breast, cut into
    ½-inch strips
½ cup red wine
1 teaspoon salt
1 teaspoon ground red
    pepper
1 tablespoon reduced-
    calorie margarine
2 cups fresh broccoli florets

2 cups fresh
    cauliflowerettes
1 large carrot, thinly sliced
    (1 cup)
½ cup finely chopped red
    bell pepper
¼ teaspoon ground
    turmeric
¼ teaspoon ground sage
1½ cups water
1 teaspoon cornstarch

In a large glass bowl, combine the turkey, wine, salt and red pepper and mix well. Cover and refrigerate overnight to marinate.

Melt the margarine in a medium skillet over high heat. Add the turkey and next 6 ingredients; cook for 10 minutes, stirring often. Dissolve the cornstarch in the water. Add to the skillet. Cover and cook 5 minutes longer or until vegetables are crisp-tender.

PER SERVING	KCAL	FATgm	CHOLmg	SODmg
	183	2	76	509

Turkey and Tortilla Meat Pie

*T*his recipe calls for a can of tomatoes with chilies. If such a product is not available in your area, substitute with a mixture made from one small can of chili peppers and one can of whole tomatoes.

MAKES 6 SERVINGS

1 pound ground turkey breast
1 cup chopped onions
½ cup chopped bell pepper
½ cup chopped celery
3 plum tomatoes, peeled, seeded and chopped
One 10-ounce can tomatoes with chilies

One 16-ounce can hot chili beans, rinsed and drained
One 10-ounce can reduced-calorie cream of mushroom soup
½ cup shredded reduced-fat Cheddar cheese
Six 6-inch tortillas

Preheat the oven to 350°F.

Spray the inside of a medium skillet with nonstick vegetable cooking spray and place over high heat. Add the turkey and sauté for 10 minutes, or until browned. Add the onions, bell pepper and celery and cook for 15 minutes, stirring often. Add the fresh and canned tomatoes; cook and stir for 10 minutes. Add the drained beans and mushroom soup; cook, stirring, 5 minutes longer.

Spray the inside of a 9-inch-square baking dish with nonstick vegetable cooking spray. Make a layer of tortillas, then a layer of the meat mixture. Repeat the process until all the ingredients are used. Top with the cheese and bake 15 minutes.

PER SERVING	KCAL	FATgm	CHOLmg	SODmg
	199.60	2.16	66.33	708.55

Smoked Turkey Sausage

A*ndouille is the most popular Cajun smoked pork sausage, but turkey sausage is much lower in fat and calories, so I use it in all my low-calorie recipes. Turkey sausage is now available in supermarkets, but if you would like to try your hand at making your own, here's how. You can also buy turkey sausage and smoke it yourself.*

I've included two methods for making sausage, one using sausage casings (small quantities are readily available in many supermarkets), the other using aluminum foil.

MAKES ABOUT 3 POUNDS

3½ pounds skinned and
    boned turkey breast
½ pound potatoes, peeled
    and quartered
1 teaspoon salt
1 tablespoon paprika
1½ teaspoons ground red
    pepper

1 teaspoon ground white
    pepper
1 teaspoon granulated
    garlic
½ teaspoon ground sage
¼ teaspoon ground nutmeg
2 teaspoons Liquid Smoke
Sausage casings

Following the manufacturer's directions, light the smoker; cover and allow the heat and smoke to accumulate.

In a meat grinder or food processor, grind together the turkey and potatoes until coarsely ground. Transfer to a mixing bowl and add all the remaining ingredients *except* the casings, mixing thoroughly. Refrigerate until ready to use.

SAUSAGE CASINGS METHOD: Soak the sausage casings for 1 hour in a small bowl with enough water to cover. Rinse the casings thoroughly to remove the excess salt. Running water through the casings will reveal if there are any holes in them. If holes or leaks are found, discard the casing. Place one of the casings on a sausage horn stuffer, taking care not to tear it. Tie a knot in the other end and stuff the casing with the turkey mixture. When stuffed, tie a knot to seal the open end. Place the sausage on the rack in the smoker and smoke for 2 hours. Turn the sausage and smoke for an additional 2 hours.

ALUMINUM FOIL METHOD: Tear off two 20-inch pieces of aluminum foil. Place half of the turkey mixture lengthwise on each piece of foil, 3 inches in from the edge. Roll the foil tightly to form a log. Place the sausage on the rack in the smoker and smoke for 2 hours, turning every 20 to 30 minutes to cook on all sides. Remove the sausage from the smoker and carefully remove the foil. Smoke the sausage without the foil for an additional 2 hours, turning the sausage every 20 minutes or so to smoke evenly. When the sausage is done, you can eat it as is or use as directed in my recipes. The sausage can be refrigerated or frozen until ready to use.

PER ½ POUND	KCAL	FATgm	CHOLmg	SODmg
	340	2	189	120

BEEF, PORK AND OTHER MEATS

Moss Street Sirloin

I *purchase most of my beef from a little butcher shop on Moss Street, which is not far from my home. So—that's how this recipe got its name!*

MAKES 6 SERVINGS

½ teaspoon salt
¼ teaspoon dried oregano
  leaves, crushed
¼ teaspoon ground black
  pepper
1 pound boneless beef
  sirloin steak, about ½
  inch thick
2 tablespoons all-purpose
  flour
1 cup finely chopped onions
½ cup finely chopped green
  bell pepper

½ cup finely chopped red
  bell pepper
½ cup thinly sliced fresh
  mushrooms
1 cup red wine
½ cup water
½ cup evaporated skim
  milk
3 cups hot cooked rice or
  pasta

Sprinkle the salt, oregano and black pepper over the meat. Sprinkle flour over the meat and toss to coat well.

Spray the inside of a large skillet with nonstick vegetable cooking spray; place over high heat until very hot. Add the meat and sear for 5 minutes, turning often to prevent burning. Remove the skillet from the heat. Spray again with the cooking spray and return to the heat. Cook 10 minutes longer. Add the next 6 ingredients and continue cooking for 10 minutes, turning often. Add the milk; cook and stir 5 minutes more, or until the sauce thickens. Serve over rice or pasta.

PER SERVING	KCAL	FATgm	CHOLmg	SODmg
	251	9.3	68	265

Smothered Steak

To "smother" means to cover, and this recipe is covered and cooked with the good flavors of the onions and bell peppers. Everyone has a personal version of how steak should be cooked, but this recipe is guaranteed to "smother" you with compliments!

MAKES 2 SERVINGS

½ teaspoon salt-free lemon-pepper seasoning
¼ teaspoon salt
½ pound boneless top round steak
1 cup chopped onions
½ cup chopped green bell pepper

½ cup chopped red bell pepper
1 teaspoon cornstarch
¼ teaspoon browning and seasoning sauce
1½ cups water
1 cup hot cooked rice

Sprinkle the lemon-pepper seasoning and salt over the meat. Spray the inside of a large skillet with nonstick vegetable cooking spray and place over high heat. Add the meat and sear for 5 minutes, or until it is browned. Add the onions and bell peppers; cook, stirring, for 5 minutes. Dissolve the cornstarch and browning and seasoning sauce in the water and add to the skillet. Reduce heat to medium and cook, covered, for 15 minutes, stirring often. Serve over rice.

PER SERVING	KCAL	FATgm	CHOLmg	SODmg
	256	7.4	92	328

Steak and Tomatoes

MAKES 4 SERVINGS

½ teaspoon ground white
   pepper
½ teaspoon ground oregano
½ teaspoon dried basil
   leaves, crushed
½ teaspoon chili powder
½ teaspoon paprika
1 pound boneless round
   steak
½ cup finely chopped
   onions

½ cup finely chopped bell
   pepper
1 cup water
One 16-ounce can salt-free
   whole tomatoes,
   chopped
¼ teaspoon browning and
   seasoning sauce

In a small bowl, combine the first 5 ingredients and mix well. Sprinkle the seasoning mix over both sides of the meat.

Spray the inside of a large skillet with nonstick vegetable cooking spray and place over high heat. Add the meat and sear for 3 minutes on each side, or until browned. Add the onions and bell pepper; cook and stir for 5 minutes. Add the water, tomatoes (with their juice) and browning sauce. Cover and cook 20 minutes longer, stirring occasionally.

PER SERVING	KCAL	FATgm	CHOLmg	SODmg
	232	7.3	92	81

Stuffed Rolled Steak

½ teaspoon salt
½ teaspoon onion powder
½ teaspoon granulated garlic
½ teaspoon ground white pepper
½ teaspoon celery seed
½ teaspoon ground savory
1 pound boneless beef round steak
1 tablespoon low-sodium Worcestershire sauce
1 cup finely chopped onions
1 cup finely chopped green bell pepper

1 cup finely chopped red bell pepper
½ cup thinly sliced fresh mushrooms
1 teaspoon sugar
1 tablespoon all-purpose flour
1½ cups water
½ cup red wine
¼ teaspoon browning and seasoning sauce
8 small new potatoes, peeled
2 small carrots, quartered

Combine the first 6 ingredients in a small bowl. Mix well and sprinkle over both sides of the meat. Sprinkle with the Worcestershire sauce and refrigerate for 1 hour to marinate.

Spray the inside of a large skillet with nonstick vegetable cooking spray and place over high heat. Add *half* of the onions and *half* of both bell peppers, reserving the remaining onions and bell peppers for later use; sauté for 5 minutes. Add the mushrooms and cook for 3 minutes, stirring often.

Remove from the heat and let cool to the touch. Spoon the sautéed vegetables down the center of the marinated meat. Roll the steak, jelly-roll fashion, and tie with cooking string.

Spray the inside of a 5-quart Dutch oven with nonstick vegetable cooking spray and place over high heat. Add the meat and sugar; cook and stir for 5 minutes, or until the meat is browned. Add the remaining onions and bell peppers; cook and stir for 3 minutes. Dissolve the flour in the water and add to the pot along with the wine and browning sauce; cook for 10 minutes, stirring often. Add the potatoes and carrots; cover and cook for 20 minutes, or until meat is tender, stirring occasionally.

PER SERVING	KCAL	FATgm	CHOLmg	SODmg
	246	7	51	332

One-Skillet Sirloin and Vegetables

I created this dish for the working mothers of the world. It's great for those busy days and leaves only one skillet to clean!

MAKES 4 SERVINGS

Two 14-ounce cans
  artichoke hearts,
  drained
2 tablespoons balsamic
  vinegar
2 tablespoons salt-free beef
  bouillon granules
2 cups water
½ pound beef sirloin steak,
  cut into 1-inch cubes
3 small dried hot chili
  peppers, crushed

1 tablespoon low-sodium
  soy sauce
½ teaspoon salt
½ roasted large green bell
  pepper (page 220),
  thinly sliced
½ roasted large red bell
  pepper, thinly sliced
1 small onion, cut in half
  and thinly sliced
½ cup broccoli florets
½ cup cauliflowerettes

In a medium bowl, combine the artichoke hearts and vinegar; set aside. Dissolve the bouillon granules in *1 cup* of the water and set aside. Spray the inside of a large skillet with nonstick vegetable cooking spray and place over high heat. Add the meat and sauté for 5 minutes. Add the chili peppers, soy sauce and salt; continue cooking. Stir in the dissolved bouillon and cook for 10 minutes. Add the remaining water and all the remaining ingredients. Cover and cook for 5 minutes. Uncover and cook 5 minutes longer, stirring often.

PER SERVING	KCAL	FATgm	CHOLmg	SODmg
	183	6.6	52	495

Stir-fried Beef

MAKES 6 SERVINGS

2 tablespoons low-sodium
    soy sauce
1 teaspoon granulated
    garlic
½ teaspoon ground ginger
¼ teaspoon salt
¼ teaspoon ground white
    pepper
¼ teaspoon ground red
    pepper
1 pound beef flank steak,
    cut into 1-inch strips

1 tablespoon salt-free beef
    bouillon granules
2 teaspoons cornstarch
1 cup water
1 medium onion, thinly
    sliced and separated
    into rings
½ green bell pepper, thinly
    sliced
½ red bell pepper, thinly
    sliced
2 cups fresh broccoli florets

Sprinkle the soy sauce, garlic, ginger, salt, white pepper and red pepper over the meat; mix well. Dissolve the bouillon granules and cornstarch in the water and set aside. Spray the inside of a large skillet with nonstick vegetable cooking spray and place over high heat. Add the meat and sauté for 15 minutes, or until browned. Add the onion, bell peppers and broccoli; cook and stir for 5 minutes. Stir in the dissolved cornstarch. Cook, stirring, 5 minutes longer, or until the vegetables are crisp-tender.

PER SERVING	KCAL	FATgm	CHOLmg	SODmg
	204	8.9	70	255

Sam's Cubed Beef in Brown Gravy

Known in the South as grillades, this dish can be served many ways. It can be served over hot cooked rice or pasta, and in New Orleans some restaurants even serve it with grits for breakfast.

MAKES 4 SERVINGS

1 pound boneless beef chuck steak, cut into 1-inch cubes
½ teaspoon granulated garlic
½ teaspoon ground white pepper
½ teaspoon ground red pepper

¼ teaspoon salt
¼ teaspoon dried thyme
1 cup finely chopped onions
1 cup finely chopped fresh mushrooms
½ cup water
½ cup white wine
2 cups hot cooked rice or pasta

Spray the inside of a medium skillet with nonstick vegetable cooking spray and place over high heat. Add the cubed beef and next 5 ingredients; cook, stirring, for 15 minutes. Add the onions, mushrooms, water and wine. Reduce the heat to medium, cover and cook for 30 minutes, or until the meat is tender. Serve hot over rice or pasta.

PER SERVING	KCAL	FATgm	CHOLmg	SODmg
	258	7.3	92	218

Beef Curry

*C*urry powder is a blend of as many as 16 to 20 ground spices.

Makes 4 servings

¼ teaspoon salt
¼ teaspoon ground red
    pepper
1 pound boneless beef
    round steak, cut into
    1-inch cubes
1 tablespoon low-sodium
    Worcestershire sauce

1 cup chopped onions
1 cup water
½ cup stewed tomatoes
½ teaspoon curry powder
¼ cup finely chopped green
    onions
2 cups hot cooked rice

Sprinkle the salt and red pepper over the meat and mix well. Spray the inside of a large skillet with nonstick vegetable cooking spray and place over high heat. Add the meat and Worcestershire sauce; cook, stirring, for 5 minutes, or until browned. Add the onions and cook and stir for 5 minutes. Add the water, tomatoes and curry powder. Reduce the heat, cover and cook for 15 minutes, stirring occasionally. Add the green onions; remove from the heat and let stand 10 minutes before serving. Serve over rice.

PER SERVING	KCAL	FATgm	CHOLmg	SODmg
	245	7.2	92	296

Beef Fajitas

MAKES 6 SERVINGS

FOR THE FILLING
2½ teaspoons chili powder
½ teaspoon granulated garlic
¼ teaspoon salt
⅛ teaspoon ground cumin
⅛ teaspoon ground sage
1 pound beef flank steak, cut into ¼-inch strips

FOR THE SAUCE
1 cup finely chopped onions
2 cloves garlic, minced
1 jalapeño pepper, very finely chopped

3 medium tomatoes, peeled, seeded and chopped
1 cup water
2 teaspoons quick-mixing flour
1 teaspoon chili powder
1 teaspoon ground oregano
½ teaspoon salt

6 corn tortillas
½ cup shredded part-skim mozzarella cheese

To PREPARE THE BEEF FILLING: In a small bowl, combine first 5 ingredients; mix well and sprinkle over the beef. Spray the inside of a medium cast-iron skillet with nonstick vegetable cooking spray and place over high heat. Add the meat and sauté for 5 minutes, or until browned on all sides. Set aside.

To PREPARE THE SAUCE: Spray the inside of a medium saucepan with nonstick vegetable cooking spray and place over medium heat. Add the onions, garlic and jalapeño pepper; sauté for 10 minutes. Add the remaining sauce ingredients and cook 15 minutes longer, stirring often. Set aside.

To Prepare the Tortillas: Spray the inside of a heavy skillet with nonstick vegetable cooking spray. Place over high heat and brown the tortillas one at a time, about 1 minute per side.

To Assemble: Preheat the oven to 350°F. Spray the inside of an 8-inch-square baking dish with nonstick vegetable cooking spray and set aside. Spoon equal amounts of the beef filling down the center of each tortilla; fold the tortillas in thirds and place seam side down in the baking dish. Pour the sauce over the tortillas and top with the cheese. Bake for 10 minutes, or until cheese is melted.

PER SERVING	KCAL	FATgm	CHOLmg	SODmg
	255	7.1	61	397

Beef Tamales

These great-tasting tamales can be served as a main meal or as an appetizer. Serve with Spanish Rice (page 271) or Taco Rice (page 274).

MAKES 15 SERVINGS

15 dried corn husks
1 pound lean ground beef
½ cup finely chopped onions
½ teaspoon salt
½ teaspoon granulated garlic
3¾ cups beef stock
1½ cups masa harina

¼ cup reduced-calorie margarine
1 tablespoon olive oil
2 tablespoons all-purpose flour
3 dried hot chili peppers, crushed
2 tablespoons plus ½ teaspoon chili powder

Simmer the husks in water to cover for 15 minutes. Weight with a heatproof plate to keep them submerged. Remove from the heat and let stand in the water for a couple of hours, or until the husks are pliable. Separate the husks and pat dry with paper towels; set aside.

Spray the inside of a medium skillet with nonstick vegetable cooking spray and place over high heat. Add the meat and sauté for 5 minutes. Add the onions, salt and garlic; cook, stirring, for 10 minutes. Stir in ½ cup of the stock and cook, stirring, 10 minutes longer, or until all the liquid has evaporated. Remove from the heat and set aside.

In a medium bowl, combine the masa harina and margarine; mix with a fork until the mixture resembles bread crumbs. Slowly stir in 1¼ cups of the stock, mix well and set aside.

Heat the oil in a medium saucepan over high heat. Add the flour and cook for 5 minutes, or until it is light brown, stirring constantly. Stir in the remaining *2 cups* of stock, the chili peppers and chili powder; cook and stir for 10 minutes. Spoon the meat mixture into the saucepan. Reduce the heat to a simmer; cover and cook 10 minutes longer, or until all liquid has evaporated, stirring often. Remove from the heat and set aside.

To Assemble the Tamales: Lay out a lightly dried corn husk with the tapering end toward you. Spread a portion of the dough (about 3 tablespoons) into a 4-inch square on the corn husk. Spoon 2 tablespoons of the meat filling down the center of the dough. Pick up the 2 long sides of the corn husk and bring them together (this will make the dough surround the filling). Fold up one end of the husk (empty of filling) to form a "bottom," leaving the other end open. Repeat the process with remaining ingredients. Put the tamales on a wire rack; put the wire rack inside a large saucepan with 2 cups of water and bring to a boil over high heat. Cover and steam the tamales for 15 minutes.

PER SERVING	KCAL	FATgm	CHOLmg	SODmg
	163	6.2	27	134

Beef and Vegetables

This dish is great served alone or with hot cooked rice or pasta. I like them all!

MAKES 4 SERVINGS

1½ cups water
4 ounces whole baby
    carrots (about 1 cup)
½ pound boneless beef
    round steak
1 tablespoon low-sodium
    soy sauce
1 small onion, thinly sliced
    and separated into
    rings
½ green bell pepper, thinly
    sliced

½ red bell pepper, thinly
    sliced
2 cups cauliflowerettes
2 cups broccoli florets
2 tablespoons salt-free
    lemon-pepper
    seasoning
½ teaspoon salt
¼ teaspoon ground red
    pepper

In a small saucepan over high heat, bring *1 cup* of the water to a boil. Add the carrots and cook for 12 minutes, or until the carrots are tender; drain and set aside.

Spray the inside of a large skillet with nonstick vegetable cooking spray and place over high heat. Add the meat and sauté for 10 minutes, or until browned. Add the soy sauce and cook for 5 minutes. Add the next 5 ingredients; cook and stir for 2 minutes. Add the drained carrots, the remaining ½ cup water and the seasonings. Cook and stir 15 minutes longer.

PER SERVING	KCAL	FATgm	CHOLmg	SODmg
	182	6.3	51	319

Beef Enchiladas

¼ teaspoon salt
½ pound beef flank steak,
*   cut into ½-inch strips*
1 cup low-fat cottage cheese
2 tablespoons evaporated
*   skim milk*
2 teaspoons lemon juice
One 10½-ounce can
*   reduced-calorie cream*
*   of mushroom soup*

2 tomatoes, peeled, seeded
*   and chopped*
2 tablespoons sliced
*   jalapeño pepper*
¼ cup shredded reduced-fat
*   Cheddar cheese*
Four 6" flour tortillas

Preheat the oven to 350°F.

Sprinkle the salt over the meat and mix well. Place the cottage cheese, milk and lemon juice in a blender and process until smooth; set aside. Spray the inside of a medium skillet with non-stick vegetable cooking spray and place over high heat. Add the meat and sauté for 2 minutes, or until browned on all sides. Remove from the heat. Transfer the meat to a plate and set aside.

Spray the same skillet again with the cooking spray and place over medium heat. Add the mushroom soup, tomatoes, jalapeño and blended cottage cheese. Cook and stir for 2 minutes. Add *2 tablespoons* of the Cheddar cheese and stir until it is melted. Remove from the heat.

Dip each tortilla in the sauce mixture. Put equal portions of meat in the center of each tortilla, then spoon equal portions of sauce over the meat. Fold the tortillas in thirds and place seam side down in a 9-inch-square baking dish. Top with the remaining Cheddar cheese. Bake for 20 minutes.

PER SERVING	KCAL	FATgm	CHOLmg	SODmg
	311	9.5	56	490

Pan-Sautéed Veal

¼ teaspoon salt
¼ teaspoon ground red
    pepper
¼ teaspoon paprika
½ pound boneless veal,
    thinly sliced
¼ cup all-purpose flour
½ cup finely chopped
    onions
¼ cup finely chopped green
    bell pepper

¼ cup finely chopped red
    bell pepper
1½ cups water
1 tablespoon salt-free beef
    bouillon granules
2 tablespoons reduced-
    calorie soft-style cream
    cheese

Sprinkle the salt, red pepper and paprika over both sides of the meat; dredge through the flour and set aside. Spray the inside of a large skillet with butter-flavored nonstick vegetable cooking spray and place over high heat. Add the meat and sauté for 2 minutes on each side, or until browned, turning often to prevent burning. Transfer the meat to a platter; keep warm.

To the same skillet, add the onions, bell peppers and ½ cup of the water. Cook and stir for 5 minutes. Dissolve the bouillon granules in the remaining water and add to the skillet. Reduce the heat to a simmer; cook for 15 minutes, stirring often. Stir in the cream cheese and cook for 5 minutes. Remove from the heat and spoon the sauce over the meat.

PER SERVING	KCAL	FATgm	CHOLmg	SODmg
	429	23.2	119	437

Two-Pepper Pork Chops

This dish can be served over rice or pasta.

MAKES 6 SERVINGS

½ teaspoon salt
¼ teaspoon ground white
   pepper
¼ teaspoon ground red
   pepper
1 pound lean pork chops,
   thinly sliced
1 tablespoon salt-free beef
   bouillion granules
1 cup water
2 tablespoons balsamic
   vinegar

2 tablespoons Dijon
   mustard
2 tablespoons honey
1 tablespoon cornstarch
¼ cup finely chopped onion
¼ cup finely chopped green
   bell pepper
¼ cup finely chopped red
   bell pepper

Sprinkle the seasonings over the pork chops. Spray the inside of a medium skillet with nonstick vegetable cooking spray and place over medium heat. Add the pork chops a few at a time and cook for 2 to 3 minutes, or until browned on both sides, turning often. Remove the pork chops and set aside.

In a small bowl, dissolve the bouillon granules in the water. Add the vinegar, mustard, honey and cornstarch, stirring well; set aside.

To same skillet over medium heat, add the onion and bell peppers; cook and stir for 3 minutes. Turn the heat to high; add the pork chops and bouillon mixture. Cook and stir 15 minutes longer.

PER SERVING	KCAL	FATgm	CHOLmg	SODmg
	234	12.4	73	294

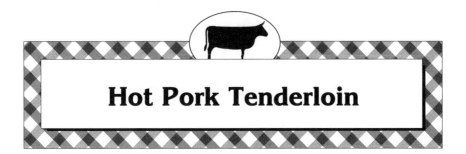

Hot Pork Tenderloin

MAKES 4 SERVINGS

1 pound boneless pork
    tenderloin
2 tablespoons balsamic
    vinegar
2 tablespoons lime juice
1 teaspoon crushed dried
    chili peppers
1/2 teaspoon salt
1/4 teaspoon ground white
    pepper
1/4 teaspoon ground cumin

1/4 teaspoon dried oregano
    leaves, crushed
1/4 teaspoon ground red
    pepper
1 cup chopped onions
1 tablespoon salt-free beef
    bouillon granules
1/2 cup water
One 10-ounce can whole
    tomatoes with green
    chilies

Place the meat in a medium bowl and add the vinegar and lime juice. Combine the next 6 ingredients in a small bowl; mix well and sprinkle over the meat. Refrigerate for 30 minutes to marinate.

Spray the inside of a 5-quart Dutch oven with nonstick vegetable cooking spray and place over high heat. Add the marinated meat and onions; sauté for 10 minutes, or until the meat is browned. Dissolve the bouillon granules in the water and add to the pot along with the tomatoes, stirring well. Cook for 15 minutes, stirring often and mashing the tomatoes with a spoon. Remove from the heat; transfer the meat to a platter and spoon the sauce over it.

PER SERVING	KCAL	FATgm	CHOLmg	SODmg
	241	6.5	107	330

Pork Chops with Gingersnap Gravy

1 teaspoon paprika
½ teaspoon salt
½ teaspoon ground white
    pepper
½ teaspoon ground black
    pepper
⅛ teaspoon dry mustard
⅛ teaspoon celery seed
⅛ teaspoon ground
    coriander
⅛ teaspoon ground nutmeg
1 pound lean pork chops,
    cut ¼ inch thick

1 tablespoon salt-free beef
    bouillon granules
1½ cups water
1 cup chopped onions
½ cup chopped green bell
    pepper
½ cup chopped red bell
    pepper
4 gingersnap cookies
3 cups hot cooked rice

Combine the first 8 ingredients in a small bowl. Mix well and sprinkle over both sides of the pork chops. Dissolve the bouillon granules in the water and set aside. Spray the inside of a large skillet with nonstick vegetable cooking spray and place over medium heat. Add the pork chops and sauté for 2 minutes on each side, turning often. Add the onions, bell peppers and *1 cup* of the dissolved bouillon; cook, stirring, for 15 minutes.

Add the remaining bouillon and the gingersnaps. Cook and stir until the gingersnaps are dissolved. Serve over cooked rice.

PER SERVING	KCAL	FATgm	CHOLmg	SODmg
	235	12.9	72	245

Pork Chops in Sherry Sauce

This dish is easy to prepare, and the delicate sherry sauce adds the finishing touch!

Makes 4 servings

¼ teaspoon salt
¼ teaspoon garlic powder
¼ teaspoon ground white pepper
¼ teaspoon chili powder
¼ teaspoon paprika
1 pound boneless pork chops
½ green bell pepper, thinly sliced
½ red bell pepper, thinly sliced

½ red onion, cut in half and thinly sliced
2 tablespoons salt-free beef bouillon granules
1 tablespoon all-purpose flour
1 cup water
2 tablespoons balsamic vinegar
1 tablespoon cream sherry

Combine the first 5 ingredients in a small bowl and mix well. Sprinkle over both sides of the pork chops. Spray the inside of a large skillet with nonstick vegetable cooking spray and place over high heat. Add the pork chops; reduce the heat to medium and sauté for 10 minutes, or until browned on both sides, turning often. Remove the chops from the skillet and keep warm.

To the same skillet, add the bell peppers and onion; cook, stirring, for 5 minutes, or until crisp-tender. Transfer to a platter. Dissolve the bouillon granules and flour in the water. Spray the skillet again with cooking spray; add the dissolved bouillon and bring to a boil. Stir in the vinegar and sherry and cook 10 minutes longer. Spoon the sauce over the pork chops.

PER SERVING	KCAL	FATgm	CHOLmg	SODmg
	112	2.9	53	164

Pork Chops in Cream Sauce

*P*ork chops can be prepared in many ways, and in the South, we've probably tried them all. I hope you enjoy this low-fat version!

1 tablespoon salt-free
   lemon-pepper
   seasoning
½ teaspoon salt
½ teaspoon granulated
   garlic
½ teaspoon ground white
   pepper
½ teaspoon chili powder
½ teaspoon paprika
1 pound boneless pork
   chops

1 cup chopped onions
½ cup chopped green bell
   pepper
½ cup chopped red bell
   pepper
½ cup chopped celery
1½ cups salt-free chicken
   broth
2 teaspoons cornstarch
1 cup evaporated skim milk

In a small bowl, combine the first 6 ingredients. Mix well and re-serve *1 tablespoon* for later use. Sprinkle the remaining seasoning mix over both sides of the pork chops. Spray the inside of a large skillet with nonstick vegetable cooking spray and place over high heat. Add the chops and sauté for 5 minutes, or until browned on both sides, turning often to prevent burning. Remove the chops and keep warm.

   Spray the same skillet again with the cooking spray and place over high heat. Add the onions, bell peppers and celery; cook, stirring, for 5 minutes. Add the broth and the reserved seasoning

mix; cover, reduce the heat to medium and cook for 10 minutes, stirring often.

Dissolve the cornstarch in the milk and add to the skillet. Cook and stir 10 minutes longer, or until the sauce thickens. Serve over the pork chops.

PER SERVING	KCAL	FATgm	CHOLmg	SODmg
	184	8.9	55	210

Stuffed Pork Loin

This dish is a must for special occasions. It can be prepared a day ahead and refrigerated until ready to bake.

MAKES 6 SERVINGS

1 pound boneless pork loin
½ cup sweet red wine
2 teaspoons granulated garlic
1 teaspoon salt
1 teaspoon hot dry mustard
½ teaspoon ground red pepper
2 cups fresh chopped spinach
1 cup thinly sliced fresh mushrooms
½ medium green bell pepper, thinly sliced

½ medium red bell pepper, thinly sliced
1 fresh jalapeño pepper, thinly sliced
1 tablespoon salt-free beef bouillon granules
1 teaspoon cornstarch
1 cup water
⅓ cup very finely chopped onion
⅓ cup very finely chopped green bell pepper
⅓ cup very finely chopped red bell pepper

Butterfly the pork loin and set aside. In a medium bowl, combine the wine, garlic, salt, mustard and red pepper; add the meat and refrigerate for 1 hour.

In a medium bowl, combine the spinach, mushrooms, sliced bell peppers and jalapeño. Remove the marinated meat from its bowl and pour the marinade over the spinach mixture; toss well.

Preheat the oven to 375°F.

Place the meat on a clean flat surface. Spoon the spinach mixture down the center of the meat, then roll up the meat, jelly-roll fashion, and tie with cooking string. Place the meat in a loaf pan that has been sprayed with nonstick vegetable cooking spray. Dissolve the bouillon granules and cornstarch in the water and pour into the loaf pan. Cover with aluminum foil and bake for 30 minutes. Uncover, baste the meat with the pan juices, and add the onion and chopped bell peppers. Cover and bake 20 minutes longer. Serve hot.

PER SERVING	KCAL	FATgm	CHOLmg	SODmg
	230	10.7	71	422

Pork Loin with Curry Sauce

Stuffed pork loin alone is truly out of this world, but when combined with a delicate curry sauce, it's simply a masterpiece!

MAKES 6 SERVINGS

1 pound boneless pork loin
1 tablespoon low-sodium
    Worcestershire sauce
½ teaspoon salt
½ teaspoon granulated
    garlic
½ teaspoon ground white
    pepper
½ teaspoon paprika
1 small onion, cut in half
    and thinly sliced

1 small green bell pepper,
    thinly sliced
1 small red bell pepper,
    thinly sliced
¼ teaspoon curry powder
1 cup salt-free chicken
    broth
1 cup corn flakes
Curry Sauce (page 287)

Preheat the oven to 400°F.

Cut off ½ *pound* from the end of the pork loin and place in a food processor. Process into ground pork; set aside. Butterfly the pork loin and sprinkle with the Worcestershire sauce. Mix together the salt, garlic, white pepper and paprika. Sprinkle over both sides of the meat; set aside.

Spray the inside of a large skillet with butter-flavored nonstick vegetable cooking spray and place over medium heat. Add ground pork, onion, bell peppers and curry powder; cook, stirring, for 5 minutes. Add the broth and corn flakes; stir until all the liquid is absorbed. Remove from the heat and let cool for 2 to 3 minutes.

Spoon the mixture down the center of the meat. Fold in both sides of the meat and tie with cooking string. Spray the inside of a baking dish with nonstick vegetable cooking spray. Place the meat, seam side down, in the dish; cover with aluminum foil and bake for 35 minutes. Remove from the oven and remove the cooking string. Cut the pork into ½-inch-thick slices. Top with the curry sauce.

PER SERVING	KCAL	FATgm	CHOLmg	SODmg
	156	3.8	70	215

Paprika Pork Chops

A *large amount of paprika will turn the meat dark very fast. Don't be alarmed—simply remove the pork chops as soon as they darken, then proceed with the recipe.*

Makes 4 servings

1 tablespoon paprika
½ teaspoon ground red
  pepper
1 pound boneless pork
  chops, cut ¼ inch thick
2 tablespoons balsamic
  vinegar
1 tablespoon rice vinegar

2 teaspoons cornstarch
½ cup water
1 small onion, thinly sliced
1 small green bell pepper,
  thinly sliced
1 small red bell pepper,
  thinly sliced
¼ teaspoon salt

Sprinkle the paprika and red pepper over both sides of the pork chops. Place in a medium bowl and add both vinegars; let stand for 20 minutes. Dissolve the cornstarch in the water and set aside. Spray the inside of a large skillet with nonstick vegetable cooking spray and place over high heat. Add the pork chops, a few at a time, and sauté for 2 minutes on each side, turning often.

Spray the same skillet again with the cooking spray and repeat the process until all the pork chops are browned, then remove from the skillet and set aside. Add the onion and bell peppers and sauté for 1 minute. Stir in the dissolved cornstarch. Return the pork chops to the skillet; add the salt and cook 5 minutes longer, stirring often.

PER SERVING	KCAL	FATgm	CHOLmg	SODmg
	209	5.8	105	201

Pork Stir-fry

Pork is very versatile and also quite healthful when you use the right portions and cooking methods.

MAKES 2 SERVINGS

1 tablespoon salt-free beef
   bouillon granules
1 teaspoon cornstarch
1 cup water
½ pound boneless pork
   tenderloin, cut into
   ½-inch strips
1 large turnip, peeled and
   thinly sliced

½ teaspoon salt
¼ teaspoon ground red
   pepper
1 cup broccoli florets
¼ cup thinly sliced fresh
   mushrooms
2 teaspoons low-sodium soy
   sauce

In a small bowl, dissolve the bouillon granules and cornstarch in the water and set aside.

Spray the inside of a medium skillet with butter-flavored non-stick vegetable cooking spray and place over high heat. Add the meat and turnip and sauté for 10 minutes. Add the salt and red pepper; cook, stirring, for 5 minutes. Add the broccoli, mushrooms and soy sauce; continue cooking for 5 minutes. Stir in the dissolved bouillon and cornstarch. Cook and stir 5 minutes longer.

PER SERVING	KCAL	FATgm	CHOLmg	SODmg
	221	5.7	105	840

Sweet-and-Sour Pork

Makes 2 servings

2 tablespoons all-purpose
   flour
½ teaspoon salt
½ teaspoon ground red
   pepper
⅛ teaspoon ground oregano
⅛ teaspoon ground cumin
6 ounces boneless pork
   tenderloin, cut into 1-
   inch-thick rounds
1 cup unsweetened
   pineapple juice

2 tablespoons honey
1 tablespoon prepared
   mustard
1 tablespoon low-sodium
   Worcestershire sauce
1 tablespoon balsamic
   vinegar
½ cup canned unsweetened
   pineapple chunks
2 cups hot cooked pasta

In a small bowl, combine the flour, salt, red pepper, oregano and cumin; mix well. Add the pork and toss until well coated.

Spray the inside of a medium skillet with nonstick vegetable cooking spray and place over high heat. Add the pork and sauté for 5 minutes, or until browned on both sides, turning often. In a small bowl, combine the next 5 ingredients, stirring until well mixed. Pour into the skillet and reduce the heat to medium. Cook and stir for 10 minutes. Add the pineapple chunks and cook 5 minutes longer, or until the sauce thickens. Serve over the pasta.

PER SERVING	KCAL	FATgm	CHOLmg	SODmg
	506	5.5	79	676

Pork Medallions with Plum Sauce

4 pork medallions (1 ounce each)
¼ teaspoon salt
¼ teaspoon onion powder
¼ teaspoon paprika
¼ cup all-purpose flour

¼ cup water
2 plums, peeled and chopped
2 tablespoons plum preserves

Place the meat on a clean flat surface. Cover with plastic wrap and pound with a meat mallet until ¼ inch thick. Sprinkle the salt, onion powder and paprika over both sides of the meat. Dredge the meat through the flour and set aside.

Spray the inside of a large skillet with nonstick vegetable cooking spray and place over medium heat. Add the meat and sauté for 3 minutes, turning often. Spray the skillet again with the cooking spray and cook 3 minutes longer. Remove from the heat and keep warm.

To the same skillet over medium heat, add the water, plums and preserves, stirring well. Cook and stir for 5 minutes. Transfer the meat to a platter and spoon the sauce over it.

PER SERVING	KCAL	FATgm	CHOLmg	SODmg
	252	5.6	105	321

Apple and Prune Tenderloin

The *delicious blend of apples and prunes makes this dish fantastic!*

MAKES 4 SERVINGS

6 pitted prunes
¾ cup water
1 teaspoon salt
½ teaspoon garlic powder
½ teaspoon dried basil
    leaves, crushed
½ teaspoon dried cilantro
½ teaspoon ground red
    pepper
1 pound boneless pork
    tenderloin, butterflied
1 cup finely chopped onions

½ cup finely chopped celery
½ cup finely chopped
    yellow bell pepper
½ cup finely chopped green
    bell pepper
1 medium apple, peeled and
    cut in half
1 teaspoon sugar (optional)
8 small new potatoes
One 1.7-ounce jar baby
    corn, packed in water

Soak the prunes in ½ *cup* of the water overnight in the refrigerator. Drain the prunes, reserving 2 tablespoons of the liquid, and set aside.

Combine the salt, garlic powder, basil, cilantro and red pepper in a small bowl. Mix well and reserve ½ *teaspoon* for later use. Sprinkle the remaining seasoning mix over the meat and set aside. Spray the inside of a medium skillet with nonstick vegetable cooking spray and place over medium heat. Add *half* of the onions and all of the celery and bell peppers; sauté for 5 minutes.

Dice half of the apple and add to the skillet along with the drained prunes, reserved prune liquid and reserved seasoning mix. Cook and stir for 10 minutes. Remove from the heat and let cool to the touch. Spoon the mixture down the center of the meat; lift up the sides of the meat and press together (this will keep the stuffing from falling out). Tie the meat with cooking string.

Spray the inside of a 5-quart Dutch oven with nonstick vegetable cooking spray and place over medium heat. Add the meat
and sugar and sauté for 20 minutes, turning often to prevent
sticking. Slice the other half of the apple and add to the pot along
with the potatoes, corn and remaining onion; cook and stir for 5
minutes. Add the remaining ¼ cup of water and cook, covered,
5 minutes longer. Remove from the heat and let stand, covered,
5 minutes more. Place the meat on a platter and carefully remove
the cooking string. Spoon the sauce over the meat.

PER SERVING	KCAL	FATgm	CHOLmg	SODmg
	315	5.9	105	586

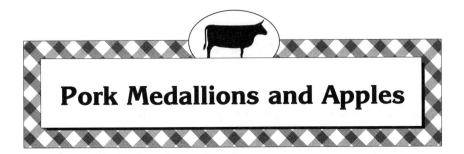

Pork Medallions and Apples

The blend of pork and sweet apples makes for a very unique dish. You can use applesauce instead of fresh apples, and the taste will still be great!

MAKES 5 SERVINGS

1 pound boneless pork
    tenderloin, cut into 5
    round medallions
½ teaspoon salt
½ teaspoon ground white
    pepper
½ teaspoon ground red
    pepper
¼ teaspoon fennel seeds
½ cup finely chopped
    onions

¼ cup finely chopped bell
    pepper
¼ cup honey
1 cup boiling water
½ teaspoon cornstarch
2 tablespoons water
2 medium apples, peeled
    and thickly sliced

Place the pork on a clean flat surface. Cover with plastic wrap and pound with a meat mallet until 1 inch thick. Combine the salt, white pepper, red pepper and fennel seeds and sprinkle over the pork.

Spray the inside of a large skillet with nonstick vegetable cooking spray and place over high heat. Add the pork and sauté for 5 minutes, or until browned on both sides, turning often. Add the onions and bell pepper; reduce the heat to medium and cook, stirring, for 10 minutes. Dissolve the honey in the boiling water. Dissolve the cornstarch in the 2 tablespoons water. Add the sliced apples to skillet along with the dissolved honey and cornstarch; cook 15 minutes longer, stirring often.

PER SERVING	KCAL	FATgm	CHOLmg	SODmg
	190	4.7	84	259

Spicy Rabbit in Red Wine Sauce

*T*his dish is sure to make your taste buds come alive! I've experimented a lot with rabbit, and discovered red wine really adds a special zing.

Makes 6 servings

2 teaspoons salt-free lemon-pepper seasoning
1½ teaspoons salt
½ teaspoon granulated garlic
½ teaspoon ground red pepper (optional)
One 2-pound rabbit, cut into 8 pieces
¼ cup all-purpose flour

2 cups chopped onions
2 bay leaves
One 4-ounce can chopped mild green chili peppers
One 16-ounce can salt-free whole tomatoes
2 cups thinly sliced fresh mushrooms
1 cup dry red wine

In a small bowl, combine the first 4 ingredients and mix well. Sprinkle over the rabbit. Place the flour on a plate and dredge the rabbit in it; set aside. Spray the inside of a 5-quart Dutch oven with nonstick vegetable cooking spray and place over high heat. Add the rabbit and sauté for 5 minutes, or until browned on all sides. Remove the rabbit and set aside.

Spray same pot again with the cooking spray. Add the onions, bay leaves and chili peppers; cook and stir for 5 minutes over high heat. Add the tomatoes, mushrooms, wine and rabbit. Cover, reduce the heat to medium, and cook for 30 minutes, stirring often.

PER SERVING	KCAL	FATgm	CHOLmg	SODmg
	280	2.9	0	568

Stuffed Rabbit Legs with Lemon-Cream Sauce

Rabbit is very low in calories and fat and can be prepared in many ways. This dish combines rabbit with a lemon sauce, which not only makes it elegant but adds a real gourmet touch.

MAKES 4 SERVINGS

4 rabbit legs, deboned
2 tablespoons balsamic
   vinegar
1 tablespoon salt-free
   lemon-pepper
   seasoning
1/2 teaspoon salt
1/2 teaspoon granulated
   garlic
1/4 teaspoon ground white
   pepper
1/4 teaspoon dried basil
   leaves, crushed
1/4 teaspoon dried oregano
   leaves, crushed
1/4 teaspoon paprika

FOR THE STUFFING
3 ounces boneless rabbit
5 ounces fresh spinach,
   chopped

1/2 cup finely chopped
   onions
1/2 cup finely chopped green
   bell pepper
1/2 cup finely chopped red
   bell pepper

FOR THE SAUCE
1 teaspoon cornstarch
1/2 cup evaporated skim
   milk
1/2 cup reserved pan juices
   from rabbit
1/4 cup reduced-calorie soft-
   style cream cheese
2 tablespoons lemon juice

3 tablespoons finely
   chopped green onions

Place the rabbit legs in a medium bowl. Add the vinegar, lemon-pepper seasoning, salt, garlic, white pepper, basil, oregano and paprika and mix well. Cover with plastic wrap and refrigerate overnight.

To Prepare the Stuffing: Preheat the oven to 400°F. Spray the inside of a large skillet with nonstick vegetable cooking spray and place over high heat. Add the meat and cook for 3 minutes, stirring often. Remove from the heat. Place the meat in a food processor and press the pulse button 2 or 3 times, or until the meat is coarsely chopped. Return the meat to the skillet and spray the skillet again with the cooking spray. Add the spinach, onions and bell peppers; cook, stirring, for 5 minutes.

Reduce the heat to medium and cook 3 minutes longer. Remove from the heat and let cool to the touch. Remove the marinated rabbit legs from the refrigerator. Spoon equal amounts of the spinach mixture inside each leg cavity; place in a 9-inch-square baking dish that has been sprayed with nonstick vegetable cooking spray. Cover with aluminum foil and bake for 30 minutes. Remove from the oven; carefully drain off the pan juices and reserve ½ cup for later use. Bake, uncovered, 15 minutes longer. Transfer to a platter and keep warm.

To Prepare the Sauce: Dissolve the cornstarch in the milk. Spray the inside of a medium skillet with nonstick vegetable cooking spray and place over high heat. Add the dissolved cornstarch and reserved pan juices; cook, stirring, for 3 minutes. When the sauce begins to thicken, remove from the heat and stir in the cream cheese and lemon juice, stirring until smooth. Spoon the sauce over the rabbit. Garnish with the green onions.

PER SERVING	KCAL	FATgm	CHOLmg	SODmg
	142	2.6	1	370

Rabbit in Brown Gravy

Rabbit is fast becoming a delicacy and can be found in most restaurants. It's great for people with cholesterol problems because it's low in fat, calories, and cholesterol. Doctors recommend it to their heart patients.

MAKES 6 SERVINGS

One 2½-pound rabbit, cut
    into serving pieces
2 cups chopped onions
½ cup chopped bell pepper
1 cup thinly sliced fresh
    mushrooms
1 cup chopped tomatoes

2 cups salt-free chicken
    broth
1 teaspoon browning and
    seasoning sauce
1 teaspoon salt
½ teaspoon ground red
    pepper

Spray the inside of a 5-quart Dutch oven with nonstick vegetable cooking spray and place over high heat. Add the rabbit and sauté for 10 minutes, stirring constantly with a wooden spoon and scraping the bottom of the pot. Add the onions and bell pepper; cook and stir for 10 minutes. Add all the remaining ingredients. Cover, reduce the heat to medium, and cook for 20 minutes, or until the rabbit is tender, stirring often.

PER SERVING	KCAL	FATgm	CHOLmg	SODmg
	171	2.1	0	367

VEGETABLES

Fresh Snap Beans with Turkey Bacon

The turkey bacon used in this great side dish gives the beans a wonderful smoky flavor.

MAKES 6 SERVINGS

4 cups water
1 pound fresh whole snap
    beans
4 small new potatoes,
    quartered
¼ cup diced turkey bacon
1 cup very finely chopped
    red onions
½ cup very finely chopped
    green bell pepper

½ cup very finely chopped
    red bell pepper
¼ cup balsamic vinegar
1 teaspoon salt
1 teaspoon granulated
    garlic
1 teaspoon ground white
    pepper

In a 5-quart Dutch oven over high heat, bring the water to a boil. Add the beans and potatoes. Cover and cook for 15 minutes, then drain, reserving *1½ cups* of the liquid. To the same pot over high heat, add the bacon and cook for 3 minutes, or until browned. (This bacon has very little fat, so stir constantly to prevent burning.)

Add the onions and bell peppers and cook for 3 minutes, stirring often. Add the beans, potatoes, reserved liquid, vinegar, salt, garlic and white pepper. Cover and cook for 15 minutes. Uncover and cook 15 minutes longer, or until the beans are tender and the liquid evaporates.

PER SERVING	KCAL	FATgm	CHOLmg	SODmg
	87	1.5	8	446

Refried Beans

This bean dish is served with just about every South-of-the-Border meal.

MAKES 4 SERVINGS

1 cup dried red beans
1 tablespoon olive oil
1 cup finely chopped onions

2 cloves garlic, minced
1 teaspoon salt

Cook the beans according to package directions, omitting the salt. When the beans are tender, drain off the liquid, reserving 1 cup.

Heat the oil in a medium saucepan over medium heat until very hot. Add the drained beans, onions, garlic and salt. Cook and stir for 10 minutes, adding the reserved liquid a little at a time. Using the back of the spoon, mash some of the beans for a creamy texture. Continue cooking for 5 minutes, or until the onions are tender and all the liquid has evaporated.

PER SERVING	KCAL	FATgm	CHOLmg	SODmg
	98	3.8	0	498

Split Peas with Canadian Bacon

7 cups water
1 pound dried split peas
½ pound Canadian bacon,
    cut into thin strips
2 cups chopped onions

¼ cup chopped green bell
    pepper
¼ cup chopped red bell
    pepper
½ teaspoon salt

In a 5-quart Dutch oven over high heat, bring the water to a boil. Add all the ingredients *except* the salt. Cover and cook for 15 minutes, stirring occasionally. Add the salt and cook 20 minutes longer, or until the peas are tender.

PER SERVING	KCAL	FATgm	CHOLmg	SODmg
	66	2.1	13	454

Creole Okra

Serve this wonderful side dish with meat, fish or poultry. Even the pickiest eaters will enjoy this okra.

MAKES 8 SERVINGS

3 pounds fresh okra, sliced
    ¼ inch thick
2 tablespoons rice vinegar
1 tablespoon balsamic
    vinegar
1½ teaspoons salt
1 teaspoon ground red
    pepper
1 pound small shrimp,
    peeled and deveined
1 cup chopped onions

½ cup chopped green bell
    pepper
½ cup chopped red bell
    pepper
¼ cup tomato paste
2 tablespoons salt-free
    chicken bouillon
    granules
4 cups water
½ cup Roux Flour (page
    289)

Spray the inside of a 5-quart Dutch oven with nonstick vegetable cooking spray and place over high heat. Add the okra and sauté for 15 minutes, stirring constantly. Add the vinegars, salt and red pepper; cook, stirring for 10 minutes. Add the shrimp, onions and bell peppers; cook and stir for 10 minutes. Dissolve the tomato paste and bouillon granules in the water and add to the pot, along with the roux flour, stirring well. Bring to a boil and cook 10 minutes longer, stirring often.

PER SERVING	KCAL	FATgm	CHOLmg	SODmg
	183	1.4	111	517

Smothered Okra

This recipe requires a good bit of stirring, but it's well worth the effort! Freeze any leftovers for another use.

MAKES 5 SERVINGS

2 pounds fresh okra, sliced
   1/4 inch thick
1 tablespoon balsamic
   vinegar
1 teaspoon salt
1 teaspoon granulated
   garlic
1/2 teaspoon ground white
   pepper

1/2 teaspoon ground red
   pepper
2 tomatoes, peeled, seeded
   and chopped
1 cup chopped onions
1/2 cup chopped green bell
   pepper
1/2 cup chopped red bell
   pepper

Spray the inside of a 5-quart Dutch oven with nonstick vegetable cooking spray and place over high heat. Add the okra and sauté for 15 minutes, or until the okra is no longer slimy. Remove from the heat and spray the surface of the okra with the cooking spray, then return the pot to high heat. Add the vinegar, salt, garlic, white pepper and red pepper; cook and stir for 10 minutes. Add the tomatoes, onions and bell peppers and stir well. Remove from the heat, spray again with the cooking spray, then return to the heat. Cook 10 minutes longer, stirring often.

PER SERVING	KCAL	FATgm	CHOLmg	SODmg
	169	1.1	0	615

Au Gratin Potatoes

*T*his is a great side dish with meat or fish. The creamy cheese taste is out of this world!

MAKES 4 SERVINGS

1 pound potatoes, peeled and thinly sliced
½ cup salt-free chicken broth
2 tablespoons dehydrated onion soup mix

Three ¾-ounce slices reduced-fat American cheese product, cut into thin strips
1 tablespoon very finely chopped fresh parsley

Preheat the oven to 450°F.

Place the potatoes in a 9-inch-square baking dish. Mix together broth and soup mix. Pour over the potatoes, then spray with butter-flavored nonstick vegetable cooking spray. Cover and bake for 20 minutes. Uncover, top with the cheese strips and bake 5 minutes longer, or until the cheese is melted. Remove from the oven and top with parsley.

PER SERVING	KCAL	FATgm	CHOLmg	SODmg
	151	3.1	0	322

Drunken Sweet Potato Pone

These sweet potatoes are not really drunk! I used amaretto liqueur for an added zip, but the potatoes are just as tasty if you decide to leave out the spirits.

MAKES 10 SERVINGS

½ cup light brown sugar
¼ cup vegetable shortening
One 4-ounce carton egg
    substitute
1 egg plus 2 egg whites
1 large sweet potato, peeled
    and shredded
1¼ cups all-purpose flour
2 teaspoons baking powder

½ teaspoon ground nutmeg
½ teaspoon ground
    cinnamon
¼ teaspoon salt
½ cup honey
1 cup evaporated skim milk
½ cup raisins
⅓ cup amaretto

Preheat the oven to 350°F.

In a medium bowl, combine the sugar, shortening, egg substitute, egg and egg whites; mix well. In a large bowl, combine the sweet potato, flour, baking powder, nutmeg, cinnamon and salt. Mix well and slowly add to egg mixture, stirring well. Dissolve the honey in the milk and add to the bowl along with the raisins and amaretto. Stir well.

Spray the inside of a 9-by-5-inch loaf pan with nonstick vegetable cooking spray. Spoon the mixture into the pan and bake for 1 hour.

PER SERVING	KCAL	FATgm	CHOLmg	SODmg
	228	6	28	174

Potato Pancakes

MAKES 6 SERVINGS

2 large potatoes, peeled and
shredded
1 small onion, peeled and
shredded
¼ teaspoon salt
¼ teaspoon ground black
pepper

3 tablespoons very finely
chopped green onions
1 tablespoon very finely
chopped fresh parsley
⅓ cup shredded reduced-fat
Cheddar cheese

Place the potato and onion in a strainer. Press out as much of their moisture as possible. Transfer to a bowl and add salt and pepper; mix well. Spray the inside of 10-inch cast-iron skillet with nonstick vegetable cooking spray and place over high heat; heat until very hot. Add the potato and onion mixture, pressing down with a fork. Reduce the heat to medium, cover and cook for 5 minutes. Using a spatula, carefully raise the potato from the edge of the skillet and spray again with cooking spray. Cook 5 minutes longer. Remove the skillet from the heat. Transfer the whole potato pancake to a plate. Spray the skillet again with cooking spray and place over medium heat. Add the potato pancake, cooked side up, and mash with fork. Add the green onions and parsley; cook, covered, 5 minutes longer. Add the cheese and cook 1 minute, or until the cheese is melted.

PER SERVING	KCAL	FATgm	CHOLmg	SODmg
	82	3.2	3	121

Grilled or Baked Herb Corn

S*erve this great side dish with meat, fish or poultry. It's perfect for outdoor barbecues.*

For a great smoky flavor, place the corn on a barbecue pit or grill and turn it several times until cooked evenly on all sides.

MAKES 4 SERVINGS

4 ears fresh corn on the cob
2 tablespoons reduced-calorie margarine, melted
2 tablespoons white wine
1 tablespoon dehydrated onion
1 tablespoon very finely chopped fresh parsley
½ teaspoon granulated garlic
½ teaspoon dried basil leaves, crushed
¼ teaspoon salt
¼ teaspoon ground white pepper
¼ teaspoon ground red pepper
¼ teaspoon chili powder

Preheat the oven to 350°F.

Shuck the corn and set aside. Combine the remaining ingredients in a small bowl and mix well. Brush the mixture all over each ear of corn. Wrap each ear in a double thickness of aluminum foil and place on a baking sheet. Bake for 30 minutes.

PER SERVING	KCAL	FATgm	CHOLmg	SODmg
	117	3.9	0	211

Baked Stuffed Turnips

An out-of-town customer tried this dish one day. She loved it so much, she often calls to check if it's on the menu. When it is, she's sure to make a special trip.

MAKES 4 SERVINGS

6 cups water
4 medium turnips
¼ cup very finely chopped yellow bell pepper
¼ cup very finely chopped red bell pepper
¼ cup very finely chopped red onion

3 plum tomatoes, peeled, seeded and chopped
½ teaspoon salt
½ teaspoon ground white pepper

Preheat the oven to 400°F.

In a 5-quart Dutch oven over high heat, bring the water to a boil. Add the turnips and cook, covered, for 30 minutes. Drain the turnips and let cool to the touch. Using a spoon, carefully scoop out center of each turnip, leaving a ½-inch shell; reserve the turnip pulp.

Spray the inside of a medium skillet with butter-flavored non-stick vegetable cooking spray and place over high heat. Add the bell peppers and onion; sauté for 3 minutes. Add the tomatoes, salt and white pepper; cook and stir 3 minutes longer. Add the reserved turnip pulp, stirring well. Remove from the heat and spoon equal amounts of the mixture into each turnip shell.

Spray the inside of a 9-inch-square baking dish with butter-flavored cooking spray. Arrange the turnips in the dish. Spoon any remaining mixture around the turnips and bake for 30 minutes.

PER SERVING	KCAL	FATgm	CHOLmg	SODmg
	51	0.4	0	341

Baked Turnips with Bacon and Cheese

*T*his dish has the hearty taste of a rich au gratin.

Makes 4 servings

1 pound small fresh
   turnips, peeled and
   thinly sliced
1 small onion, thinly sliced
½ teaspoon granulated
   garlic
½ teaspoon dried basil
   leaves, crushed
¼ teaspoon salt

¼ teaspoon ground white
   pepper
4 slices turkey bacon,
   chopped
¼ cup skim milk
½ cup evaporated skim
   milk
Three ¾-ounce slices
   reduced-fat American
   cheese product

Preheat the oven to 375°F.

Spray the inside of a 9-inch-square baking dish with nonstick vegetable cooking spray. Add the turnips and layer with the onion. Combine the next 4 ingredients and sprinkle on top of the turnips, then sprinkle with the bacon. Pour the fresh skim milk over the top; cover and bake for 30 minutes.

In a small skillet over high heat, bring the evaporated milk to a boil. Add the cheese and stir constantly until melted. Pour over the turnips and continue to bake, covered, 15 minutes longer, or until the turnips are tender.

PER SERVING	KCAL	FATgm	CHOLmg	SODmg
	130	5.3	17	768

Brussels Sprouts with Dijon Mustard

My family likes Brussels sprouts, but thinks they're too plain. So, I developed this delicate, creamy sauce to use as a topping.

MAKES FOUR ½-CUP SERVINGS

1 cup low-fat cottage cheese
2 tablespoons chopped
  pimiento
1 teaspoon lemon juice
1 teaspoon Dijon mustard

4 cups water
¼ teaspoon salt
1 pound fresh Brussels
  sprouts

In a blender, process the cottage cheese until smooth. Reserve ½ cup and refrigerate the rest for another use.

In a small bowl, combine the blended cottage cheese, pimiento, lemon juice and mustard, stirring well. Set aside.

In a medium saucepan over high heat, bring the water to a boil. Add the salt and Brussels sprouts and boil for 10 minutes. Remove from the heat and reserve 1 cup of the cooking water. Continue cooking the Brussels sprouts until the remaining water evaporates. Add the blended cottage cheese mixture and cook 1 minute longer, or until the sauce is hot.

PER SERVING	KCAL	FATgm	CHOLmg	SODmg
	66	1	1	286

Sweet-and-Sour Cabbage

1 tablespoon reduced-
    calorie margarine
1 small red cabbage,
    shredded (about 6 cups)
1 small onion, thinly sliced
    and separated into
    rings

1 teaspoon caraway seed
¼ teaspoon salt
¼ teaspoon ground white
    pepper
¼ cup dark brown sugar
¼ cup balsamic vinegar
¼ cup molasses

Melt the margarine in a 5-quart Dutch oven over high heat. Add
the cabbage and onion; cover and cook for 10 minutes, stirring
often. Uncover and add the caraway seed, salt and pepper; and
cook for 5 minutes. Remove from the heat and set aside.

In a small bowl, combine the brown sugar, vinegar and molasses; stir until dissolved, then add to the cabbage and mix well.

PER SERVING	KCAL	FATgm	CHOLmg	SODmg
	148	1.8	0	175

Cabbage Rolls with Mushroom Sauce

My granddaughter Liz loves cabbage rolls but is very conscious of her weight. So I created this low-fat version for her. Now that she lives in Baton Rouge, she asks, "Maw-Maw, can you make some for me, freeze them, and send them by mail?"

MAKES 12 SERVINGS

8 cups water
12 large cabbage leaves
1 pound ground beef top
    round
1 cup finely chopped onions
½ cup finely chopped green
    bell pepper
½ cup finely chopped red
    bell pepper
½ teaspoon salt

½ teaspoon ground white
    pepper
2 cups shredded cabbage
1 tablespoon salt-free beef
    bouillon granules
1 cup water
1 cup cooked rice
Mushroom Sauce (recipe
    follows)
Paprika

Preheat the oven to 350°F.

In a large saucepan over high heat, bring the water to a boil. Place the cabbage leaves in the boiling water; cover and cook for 5 minutes. Reduce the heat and simmer, uncovered, for 5 minutes. Drain the cabbage and set aside until cool to the touch.

Spray the same saucepan with vegetable cooking spray and place over high heat. Add the meat and sauté for 5 minutes. Add the onions, bell peppers, salt and pepper; cook and stir for 10 minutes. Add the shredded cabbage and continue cooking. Dissolve the bouillon granules in the water and add to the saucepan; cook and stir for 5 minutes. Add the rice and *1 cup* of the mushroom sauce; cook, stirring, for 3 minutes. Remove from the heat and let cool to the touch.

Place the cabbage leaves on a clean flat surface. Spoon equal portions of the meat mixture across the center of each leaf. Carefully fold in thirds and place seam side down in a 9-inch-square baking dish that has been sprayed with nonstick vegetable cooking spray. Spoon the remaining mushroom sauce over the cabbage rolls. Cover with aluminum foil and bake for 20 minutes. Uncover, sprinkle with paprika and bake 10 minutes longer.

FOR THE MUSHROOM SAUCE

1 tablespoon reduced-
  calorie margarine
2 cups thinly sliced
  mushrooms
2 tablespoons all-purpose
  flour

2 cups evaporated skim
  milk
1/8 teaspoon salt
1/8 teaspoon ground white
  pepper

Melt the margarine in a medium saucepan over high heat. Add the mushrooms and sauté for 3 minutes. Add the flour; cook and stir for 2 minutes. When the flour starts to stick, add the milk, salt and pepper and bring to a boil. Reduce the heat to medium. Cook and stir for 2 minutes.

PER SERVING	KCAL	FATgm	CHOLmg	SODmg
	106	2.5	31	123

Tangy Spinach

MAKES 2 SERVINGS

½ pound fresh spinach
2 teaspoons extra virgin olive oil
½ red bell pepper, thinly sliced

½ small onion, thinly sliced
1 tablespoon balsamic vinegar
⅛ teaspoon salt

Rinse the spinach under cold water. Remove the stems and discard. Make a stack of 10 to 12 spinach leaves, then roll the leaves tightly to form a log and thinly slice. Repeat the process until all the leaves are sliced.

Heat the oil in a medium skillet over high heat until very hot. Add the bell pepper and onion and cook for 2 minutes, stirring often. Add the spinach, vinegar and salt. Cook and stir 5 minutes longer. Serve warm.

PER SERVING	KCAL	FATgm	CHOLmg	SODmg
	84	5.3	0	213

Mirliton Medley

This is a delicious main meal dish for vegetarians. It's also a terrific side dish served with meat, fish or poultry.

MAKES 3 SERVINGS

4 cups water
4 mirlitons, cut in half
2 cups broccoli florets
2 onions, diced
½ green bell pepper, diced
½ red bell pepper, diced
2 cups thinly sliced fresh
    mushrooms

1 dried hot chili pepper,
    crushed
½ teaspoon salt
¼ teaspoon dried basil
    leaves, crushed
2 medium tomatoes, peeled,
    seeded and chopped

In a 5-quart Dutch oven over high heat, bring the water to a boil. Add the mirlitons and cook for 8 minutes, or until crisp-tender. Remove from the heat and place the mirlitons in ice water for 4 minutes to cool, then peel, dice and set aside.

Spray the inside of a large skillet with nonstick vegetable cooking spray and place over high heat. Add the broccoli, onions and bell peppers and sauté for 5 minutes. Add the mushrooms, chili pepper, salt and basil; cook and stir for 5 minutes. Add the tomatoes and cook 2 minutes longer.

PER SERVING	KCAL	FATgm	CHOLmg	SODmg
	60	0.8	0	361

Marinated Carrots

This recipe is easy to prepare and versatile. It can be served as a side dish with fish, chicken or pork. It's also great on a relish tray for parties!

MAKES 4 SERVINGS

3 cups water
1 pound baby carrots
One-half 10¾-ounce can
    tomato soup
One 3½-ounce can whole
    jalapeño peppers
¼ cup white wine vinegar
2 tablespoons Dijon
    mustard
1 tablespoon low-sodium
    Worcestershire sauce

2 packets sugar substitute
1 teaspoon salt
1 small onion, thinly sliced
    and separated into
    rings
½ green bell pepper, thinly
    sliced
½ red bell pepper, thinly
    sliced

In a large saucepan over high heat, bring the water to a boil. Add the carrots and cook for 20 minutes, or until tender. Remove from the heat, drain and let cool. Put the carrots and all the remaining ingredients in a plastic bag and seal. Shake the bag to mix well. Refrigerate overnight. Drain off the marinade and serve.

PER SERVING	KCAL	FATgm	CHOLmg	SODmg
	65	0.7	0	938

Spicy Glazed Carrots

The flavors of the vinegar and chili pepper will make your taste buds come alive! Try serving as a side dish with chicken.

MAKES 4 SERVINGS

2 cups water
1 pound baby carrots
¼ teaspoon salt
1 dried hot chili pepper,
*   crushed*

1 tablespoon sugar
1 tablespoon balsamic
*   vinegar*

In a medium saucepan over high heat, bring the water to a boil. Add the carrots and salt; cover and cook for 20 minutes. Add the remaining ingredients and cook 3 minutes longer, or until all the liquid has evaporated, shaking the skillet to prevent burning. Serve immediately.

PER SERVING	KCAL	FATgm	CHOLmg	SODmg
	44	0	0	170

Carrots and Prunes

My son-in-law asked, "Who would think of cooking prunes with carrots?" But when he tasted the finished product he yelled, "This is dynamite!"

MAKES 4 SERVINGS

12 pitted prunes	½ pound baby carrots
2 packets sugar substitute	¼ teaspoon salt
1½ cups water	⅛ teaspoon ground nutmeg

In a large bowl, combine the prunes, sugar substitute and ½ cup of the water; mix well and refrigerate overnight. Drain the prunes, reserving ¼ cup of the soaking liquid.

In a medium skillet over high heat, bring the remaining 1 cup of water to a boil. Add the carrots, reserved soaking liquid and salt; cook, covered, for 20 minutes. Add the prunes and nutmeg and cook 2 minutes longer, stirring often. Remove from the heat and let stand 10 minutes before serving.

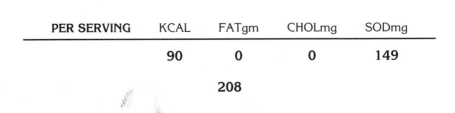

PER SERVING	KCAL	FATgm	CHOLmg	SODmg
	90	0	0	149

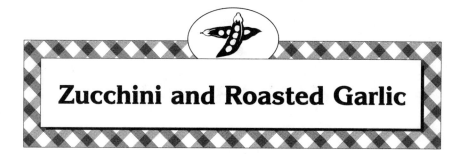

Zucchini and Roasted Garlic

I *don't eat garlic, but I still love the smell of garlic cooking. This is a great side dish with meat or fish. So here's to all you garlic lovers—enjoy!*

MAKES 4 SERVINGS

1 pound zucchini, cut into ½-inch cubes
1⅛ teaspoons salt
1 tablespoon olive oil
5 cloves garlic, cut in half
2 tablespoons chopped green onion

½ teaspoon dried oregano leaves, crushed
¼ teaspoon ground black pepper
2 tablespoons finely chopped fresh parsley
1 tablespoon lemon juice

Place the zucchini in a large glass bowl and sprinkle with *1 teaspoon* of the salt; mix well. Put the zucchini in a colander and let stand for 30 minutes, then rinse under cold water and pat dry.

Heat the oil in a medium skillet over medium heat. When hot, add the garlic and sauté for 1 minute, or until golden brown. Add the zucchini, green onion, oregano, pepper, parsley and remaining salt. Cook and stir constantly for 5 minutes, or until the zucchini is crisp-tender. Stir in the lemon juice and serve hot.

PER SERVING	KCAL	FATgm	CHOLmg	SODmg
	54	3.7	0	493

Herbed Broccoli

This side dish is one surefire way to get the kids to eat their broccoli.

3 cups water
1 pound broccoli florets
¼ cup very finely chopped
    onion
1 tablespoon reduced-
    calorie margarine
1 tablespoon salt-free
    chicken bouillon
    granules

½ teaspoon dried basil
    leaves, crushed
¼ teaspoon salt
¼ teaspoon ground white
    pepper
¼ teaspoon ground
    marjoram

In a large saucepan over high heat, bring the water to a boil. Add the broccoli and cook for 2 minutes. Using a slotted spoon, remove the broccoli and set aside. Reserve ½ cup of the water and discard the rest. In the same saucepan over high heat, bring the reserved water, onion, margarine, bouillon granules, basil, salt, pepper and marjoram to a boil; cook 1 minute. Add the broccoli and cook 1 minute longer, stirring often.

PER SERVING	KCAL	FATgm	CHOLmg	SODmg
	23	1.5	0	168

Broccoli au Gratin

MAKES 4 SERVINGS

6 cups water
4 cups broccoli florets
2 cups thinly sliced broccoli
    stems
1 cup skim milk
1 tablespoon reduced-
    calorie margarine
Two ¾-ounce slices
    reduced-fat American
    cheese product

2 ounces reduced-calorie
    processed cheese
    spread
¼ teaspoon salt
2 tablespoons chopped
    jalapeño pepper
    (optional)

Preheat the oven to 350°F.

In a 5-quart Dutch oven over high heat, bring the water to a boil. Add the broccoli and cook for 10 minutes; drain and set aside.

In a large skillet over medium heat, bring the milk and margarine to a boil. Add the next 3 ingredients; cook and stir for 3 minutes, or until cheese is melted. Add the broccoli and jalapeño; stir well.

Spray the inside of a baking dish with nonstick vegetable cooking spray. Spoon in the mixture and bake for 10 minutes.

PER SERVING	KCAL	FATgm	CHOLmg	SODmg
	164	5.9	6	622

211

Creamy Cauliflower

A *fabulous side dish, it complements anything you choose to serve it with.*

MAKES 4 SERVINGS

3 slices lean bacon
3 cups water
4 cups cauliflowerettes
1 tablespoon reduced-
    calorie margarine
1 tablespoon all-purpose
    flour
½ cup finely chopped
    onions

½ cup finely chopped red
    bell pepper
¼ teaspoon salt
1 cup evaporated skim milk
¼ cup finely chopped green
    onions

In a heavy skillet over high heat, fry the bacon until crisp. Remove the bacon and drain on paper towels, then crumble and set aside. In a large saucepan over high heat, bring the water to a boil. Add the cauliflower and cook for 10 minutes; drain and set aside.

Melt the margarine in a large skillet over medium heat. Add the flour and cook, stirring constantly, for 1 minute. Add the onions, bell pepper and salt; cook and stir for 2 minutes. Stir in the milk and cook 2 minutes longer. Add the cauliflower and green onions; reduce heat to a simmer and cook 1 minute, or until the sauce thickens. Spoon the mixture into a serving dish and top with the crumbled bacon.

PER SERVING	KCAL	FATgm	CHOLmg	SODmg
	132	4.2	7	205

Crab-Stuffed Mushrooms

Truly a culinary delight. Serve this classic appetizer at your next dinner party, and you'll be the talk of the town!

MAKES 2 SERVINGS

6 medium fresh mushrooms
½ cup very finely chopped onions
½ cup very finely chopped green bell pepper
⅓ cup very finely chopped celery
1 cup water
½ teaspoon salt

⅛ teaspoon ground white pepper
½ pound claw crabmeat, picked over
½ cup fine dry bread crumbs
2 teaspoons low-sodium Worcestershire sauce
½ teaspoon lemon juice

Preheat the oven to 350°F.

Remove the stems from the mushrooms and set aside for another purpose. Spray the inside of a small skillet with nonstick vegetable cooking spray and place over medium heat. Add the onions, bell pepper and celery and sauté for 5 minutes. Reduce the heat and add the water, salt and pepper; continue cooking for 15 minutes, stirring often. Remove from the heat and stir in all the remaining ingredients. Mix well and stuff into the mushroom caps.

Spray the inside of a small baking dish with nonstick vegetable cooking spray. Arrange the mushrooms in the dish and bake for 30 minutes.

PER SERVING	KCAL	FATgm	CHOLmg	SODmg
	248	4.3	113	1282

Chicken-Stuffed Mushrooms

Here in South Louisiana, most mushrooms are stuffed only with seafood, so when I served this dish to customers, they were surprised at how good it was. You'll find this recipe not only tasty but also inexpensive!

MAKES 5 APPETIZERS (2 MUSHROOMS PER SERVING)

10 large fresh mushrooms
2 cups water
1 pound skinned and boned
 chicken breast, cut into
 1-inch strips
¼ cup finely chopped green
 onions
¼ cup finely chopped red
 bell pepper

½ teaspoon salt
½ teaspoon granulated
 garlic
½ teaspoon ground white
 pepper
¼ teaspoon dried oregano
 leaves, crushed
½ cup corn flakes, toasted

Preheat the oven to 350°F.

Remove the stems from the mushroom caps. Mince the stems, reserving the caps for later use. In a large saucepan over high heat, bring the water to a boil. Add the chicken and cook for 5 minutes; remove the chicken, reserving ½ cup of the stock. Place the chicken in a food processor and process until finely chopped.

Spray the inside of a medium skillet with nonstick vegetable cooking spray and place over high heat. Add the chicken, green onions, bell pepper, salt, garlic, white pepper, oregano and mushroom stems; sauté for 10 minutes. Reduce the heat, stir in

the reserved stock and cook for 10 minutes. Add the corn flakes and stir well.

Remove from the heat and let cool to the touch. Spoon the mixture into each mushroom cap. Place in a baking dish that has been sprayed with nonstick vegetable cooking spray. Cover and bake for 30 minutes.

PER SERVING	KCAL	FATgm	CHOLmg	SODmg
	214	4.3	96	454

Sausage-Stuffed Mushrooms

S*erve this terrific appetizer at your next gathering and sit back and enjoy the compliments!*

I created this dish for Dr. Eassley, a good friend and customer.

Makes 4 appetizers (2 mushrooms per serving)

½ pound Smoked Turkey Sausage (page 144)

12 medium fresh mushrooms

2 slices bread (40 calories per slice)

½ cup finely chopped onions

¼ cup finely chopped green bell pepper

¼ cup finely chopped red bell pepper

1 cup salt-free chicken broth

2 tablespoons balsamic vinegar

1 tablespoon low-sodium Worcestershire sauce

½ teaspoon salt

½ teaspoon ground red pepper

Preheat the oven to 350°F.

Remove and discard the casing from the sausage. Place the sausage in a food processor and process until it resembles ground meat; set aside. Remove the stems from the mushroom caps; mince the stems, reserving the caps for later use. Place the bread in a food processor and process into crumbs.

Spray the inside of a medium skillet with nonstick vegetable cooking spray and place over high heat. Add the ground sausage, mushroom stems, onions and bell peppers; sauté for 10 minutes. Reduce the heat to medium; stir in the broth and cook for 10 minutes. Add the vinegar, Worcestershire sauce, salt, pepper and bread crumbs, stirring well. Remove from the heat and let cool to the touch.

Carefully scoop out the inside of the mushroom caps (this leaves more room for the stuffing). Spoon the sausage mixture into each mushroom cap. Place in a baking dish that has been sprayed with nonstick vegetable cooking spray. Cover and bake for 30 minutes.

PER SERVING	KCAL	FATgm	CHOLmg	SODmg
	23	1.8	95	743

Rice-Stuffed Bell Peppers

Serve alone or with vegetables for a healthful, hearty meal.

MAKES 4 SERVINGS

½ pound ground turkey breast

1 cup chopped onions

1 cup peeled and chopped tomatoes

1 cup thinly sliced fresh mushrooms

½ cup chopped green bell pepper

½ cup chopped red bell pepper

1 teaspoon salt-free lemon-pepper seasoning

¼ teaspoon salt

¼ teaspoon ground red pepper

One-half 10-ounce can 99% fat-free condensed cream of chicken soup

1 cup cooked rice

6 cups water

2 medium bell peppers

½ cup shredded reduced-fat Cheddar cheese

Preheat the oven to 350°F.

Spray the inside of a large skillet with butter-flavored nonstick vegetable cooking spray and place over high heat. Add the turkey and sauté for 5 minutes. Add the next 8 ingredients; cook and stir for 10 minutes. Add the chicken soup and rice; stir well. Remove from the heat and set aside.

In a large saucepan, bring the water to a boil over high heat. Cut the bell peppers in half and remove the seeds. Place in the boiling water and cook for 5 minutes, or until crisp-tender; drain and pat dry. Fill each bell pepper half with the rice mixture and place in a 9-inch-square baking dish that has been sprayed with nonstick vegetable cooking spray. Top with the cheese and bake for 20 minutes.

PER SERVING	KCAL	FATgm	CHOLmg	SODmg
	180	2.2	52	223

Roasted Bell Pepper

Roasting the bell pepper makes it easy to remove the skin which can sometimes leave a slightly bitter taste. It also cuts the cooking time for most recipes. You'll find that I use roasted bell peppers in a lot of recipes in this book.

The simplest way to roast bell peppers and fresh chili peppers is to use a stovetop grill, but a broiler will give the same results.

**1 large red or green bell
   pepper**

Cut the bell pepper in half lengthwise and spray it with nonstick vegetable cooking spray. Place on a very hot grill and cook until the skin of the pepper starts to blister or bubble. Reduce the heat and continue cooking until the pepper is tender. Place the bell pepper in a paper bag to cool. Remove the skin and seeds and discard.

Corn with Crabmeat and Roasted Peppers

This is a dynamite side dish that's great with grilled fish, meat or poultry.

MAKES 4 SERVINGS

2 cups water
4 plum tomatoes
1 roasted yellow bell pepper (page 220), finely chopped
1 roasted green bell pepper, finely chopped
1 roasted red bell pepper, finely chopped
One 11-ounce can salt-free yellow corn, drained

One 11-ounce can white corn, drained
1 tablespoon sweet pickle relish
¼ cup fat-free mayonnaise
1 tablespoon balsamic vinegar
¼ teaspoon dried dillweed
12 ounces fresh lump crabmeat, picked over
4 large lettuce leaves

In a large saucepan over high heat, bring the water to a boil. Add the tomatoes and cook for 1 minute, or until the tomato skins loosen. Remove from the heat, drain and let cool to the touch. Peel off the skins, remove the seeds and chop the pulp.

In a large bowl, combine the tomatoes and all the remaining ingredients *except* the crabmeat and lettuce; stir well. Carefully fold in the crabmeat. To serve, place each lettuce leaf on a plate and spoon equal portions of the crab mixture into the centers.

PER SERVING	KCAL	FATgm	CHOLmg	SODmg
	250	6.6	90	279

Meat-Stuffed Bell Peppers

Here in South Louisiana, we stuff bell peppers with meat, seafood, rice, corn—just about anything. You can use red, yellow or green bell peppers. Try combining all three to make a very colorful meal.

MAKES 6 SERVINGS

6 medium green bell
   peppers
5 cups water
1 pound lean ground beef
1 cup finely chopped onions
½ cup finely chopped celery
½ teaspoon salt
½ teaspoon dried basil
   leaves, crushed
¼ teaspoon ground black
   pepper

One 16-ounce can salt-free
   whole tomatoes
1 tablespoon low-sodium
   Worcestershire sauce
2 tablespoons low-sodium
   catsup
6 tablespoons reduced-fat
   shredded Cheddar
   cheese

Cut each bell pepper ½ inch from the top; reserving the tops. In a 5-quart Dutch oven over high heat, bring the water to a boil. Add the bell peppers and tops; boil for 12 minutes or until crisp-tender. Remove from the heat and drain. Rinse the peppers under cold water and set aside.

Preheat the oven to 350°F.

Dry the Dutch oven, then spray with nonstick vegetable cooking spray and place over high heat. Add the ground beef and next 5 ingredients; sauté for 15 minutes, or until the beef is browned. Remove 4 of the whole tomatoes from the can and coarsely chop; add to the pot. Cook and stir 10 minutes longer.

Remove from the heat and spoon equal amounts of the mixture into each bell pepper. Arrange the peppers in a 9-inch-square

baking dish that has been sprayed with nonstick vegetable cooking spray; set aside.

Place the Dutch oven over high heat and add the remaining tomatoes, Worcestershire sauce and catsup; cook and stir for 3 minutes. Remove from the heat and spoon *2 tablespoons* of the sauce over each pepper; sprinkle with the cheese and place the reserved tops over the cheese. Cover with aluminum foil and bake for 25 minutes.

PER SERVING	KCAL	FATgm	CHOLmg	SODmg
	230	9.2	71	305

CASSEROLES AND STEWS

Breakfast Casserole

This recipe can be assembled the night before, except for the egg and milk mixture.

MAKES 6 SERVINGS

3 slices bread (40 calories per slice), toasted
6 slices Canadian bacon, diced
One 4-ounce can chopped green chili peppers
½ cup shredded reduced-fat Cheddar cheese
¼ cup finely chopped green onions

One 8-ounce carton frozen egg substitute (equal to 4 eggs), thawed
½ cup evaporated skim milk
½ teaspoon salt
¼ teaspoon ground red pepper

Preheat the oven to 375°F.

Trim the crusts from the bread; cut 1 of the bread slices in half (this will make bread fit in dish). Spray the inside of a 9-inch-square baking dish with nonstick vegetable cooking spray. Place the bread in the baking dish, then layer with the bacon, peppers, cheese and green onions. Beat together the egg substitute, milk, salt and red pepper. Pour in the baking dish and bake, uncovered, for 30 minutes.

PER SERVING	KCAL	FATgm	CHOLmg	SODmg
	100	2.9	18	639

Cauliflower and Leek Casserole

This dish can be served as a main meal or as a side dish with meat or fish.

MAKES 4 SERVINGS

2 medium leeks
2½ cups water
2 cups fresh
    cauliflowerettes
2 tablespoons reduced-
    calorie margarine
¼ cup chopped red bell
    pepper
¼ cup chopped celery
1 tablespoon all-purpose
    flour

1 tablespoon balsamic
    vinegar
½ teaspoon salt
½ teaspoon ground white
    pepper
1 cup evaporated skim milk
1 cup skim milk
Two ¾-ounce slices
    reduced-fat American
    cheese product

Preheat the oven to 375°F.

Wash the leeks well and discard the green tops; chop the leek bottoms finely. In a medium saucepan over high heat, bring 2 cups of the water to a boil. Add the cauliflower and boil for 8 minutes; drain and set aside. In a medium skillet over medium heat, melt the margarine. Add the leeks and next 6 ingredients; cook and stir for 3 minutes. Add the remaining ½ cup of water; continue to cook, stirring, 3 minutes longer. Add the evaporated milk and fresh milk and stir constantly until the mixture thickens, then add the cheese and stir until melted. Remove from the heat, add the cauliflower and mix well.

Spoon the mixture into a small baking dish that has been sprayed with nonstick vegetable cooking spray and bake for 15 minutes.

PER SERVING	KCAL	FATgm	CHOLmg	SODmg
	192	5.5	4	660

Oyster Casserole

This dish is a real treat for oyster lovers! For a lighter meal, try using corn flakes instead of bread crumbs.

MAKES 4 SERVINGS

1 cup chopped onions
½ cup chopped green bell pepper
½ cup chopped red bell pepper
1 tablespoon all-purpose flour
One-half 10-ounce can reduced-calorie cream of mushroom soup

1 cup salt-free chicken broth
2 cups corn flakes
½ teaspoon ground white pepper
¼ teaspoon salt
1 pint fresh oysters with ½ cup oyster liquid
½ cup crushed corn flakes
Paprika

Preheat the oven to 350°F.

Spray the inside of a large skillet with nonstick vegetable cooking spray and place over high heat. Add the onions and bell peppers and sauté for 5 minutes. Add the flour; cook and stir for 5 minutes. Add the mushroom soup and broth, reduce the heat to medium, and cook for 10 minutes, stirring often. Add the corn flakes, white pepper and salt and stir well.

Spoon *half* of the mixture into a 9-inch-square baking dish. Layer with the oysters, then the remaining mixture. Top with crushed corn flakes and sprinkle with paprika. Bake for 20 minutes.

PER SERVING	KCAL	FATgm	CHOLmg	SODmg
	145	2.3	39	361

Tuna Casserole with Penne Pasta

If you have children, this recipe is a must! The penne pasta can be replaced by spaghetti or macaroni.

MAKES 4 SERVINGS

4½ cups water
2 cups uncooked penne
    pasta
1 cup finely chopped onions
½ cup finely chopped green
    bell pepper
½ cup finely chopped red
    bell pepper
One 10-ounce can 99% fat-
    free condensed cream of
    chicken soup
⅓ cup evaporated skim
    milk

½ teaspoon salt
½ teaspoon granulated
    garlic
½ teaspoon ground red
    pepper
One 6½-ounce can tuna
    packed in water,
    drained
Two ¾-ounce slices
    reduced-fat American
    cheese product, diced

Preheat the oven to 350°F.

In a medium saucepan over high heat, bring *4 cups* of the water to a boil. Add the penne and cook for 8 minutes, or until tender. Remove from the heat; drain and rinse the pasta under cold water and set aside.

Spray the inside of a medium skillet with nonstick vegetable cooking spray and place over high heat. Add the onions and bell peppers and sauté for 5 minutes. Stir in the remaining ½ cup

water and cook for 2 minutes. Add the next 6 ingredients and the penne; cook and stir for 3 minutes. Remove from the heat.

Spray the inside of a baking dish with nonstick vegetable cooking spray. Add *half* of the pasta mixture and *half* of the cheese. Repeat the process, then bake for 10 minutes.

PER SERVING	KCAL	FATgm	CHOLmg	SODmg
	249	4.4	18	967

Cheesy Lemon-Chicken and Rice Casserole

MAKES 4 SERVINGS

1 pound skinned and boned chicken breast, cut into thin strips
1/3 cup very finely chopped onion
1/3 cup very finely chopped green bell pepper
1/3 cup very finely chopped red bell pepper
1 teaspoon dried hot chili pepper, crushed
1/2 teaspoon browning and seasoning sauce
1/2 teaspoon ground black pepper
1/8 teaspoon dried dillweed
2 tablespoons salt-free chicken bouillon granules
2 cups water
2 tablespoons lemon juice
1 1/2 cups uncooked quick-cooking rice
Two 3/4-ounce slices reduced-fat American cheese product, cut into 1/2-inch cubes

Preheat the oven to 350°F.

Spray the inside of a large skillet with nonstick vegetable cooking spray and place over high heat. Add the chicken and sauté for 10 minutes. Add the next 7 ingredients; cook and stir for 10 minutes. Dissolve the bouillon granules in the water and add to skillet along with the lemon juice; cook 5 minutes longer. Place the rice in a 9-inch-square baking dish. Spoon chicken and onion mixture over the rice. Bake for 15 minutes.

PER SERVING	KCAL	FATgm	CHOLmg	SODmg
	334	7.8	99	315

Spicy Turkey and
Pasta Casserole

This is a hearty main dish. To make less spicy, simply reduce the amount of chili pepper.

MAKES 4 SERVINGS

½ cup finely chopped onions

½ cup finely chopped green bell pepper

½ cup finely chopped red bell pepper

¼ teaspoon salt

¼ teaspoon ground black pepper

One 12-ounce can white turkey meat

One 10½-ounce can reduced-calorie cream of mushroom soup

½ cup water

2 dried hot chili peppers, crushed

2 cups cooked pasta

2 tablespoons grated Parmesan cheese

Preheat the oven to 375°F.

Spray the inside of a medium skillet with butter-flavored non-stick vegetable cooking spray and place over high heat. Add the onions, bell peppers, salt and pepper and sauté for 10 minutes. Add the turkey meat and crumble with a fork; cook for 5 minutes. Stir in the mushroom soup, water and chili peppers and cook 5 minutes longer. Remove from the heat and add the cooked pasta, stirring well. Spray the inside of a 9-inch-square baking dish with nonstick vegetable cooking spray. Spoon the mixture into the dish and top with the cheese. Bake for 15 minutes.

PER SERVING	KCAL	FATgm	CHOLmg	SODmg
	166	2.9	2	586

Turkey and Rice Casserole

*T*his is a wonderful dish for the whole family.

*3 ounces artichoke hearts
    packed in water*
1 tablespoon lemon juice
*1 tablespoon salt-free beef
    bouillon granules*
1 cup water
*1 pound ground turkey
    breast*
1 cup finely chopped onions
½ cup finely chopped celery
*½ cup finely chopped green
    bell pepper*

½ teaspoon salt
*½ teaspoon ground red
    pepper*
*1 tablespoon low-sodium
    Worcestershire sauce*
*1 teaspoon browning and
    seasoning sauce*
2 cups cooked rice
*½ cup shredded reduced-fat
    Cheddar cheese*

Preheat the oven to 375°F.

Place the artichoke hearts and lemon juice in a small glass bowl and refrigerate for 30 minutes to marinate. Dissolve the bouillon granules in the water and set aside.

Spray the inside of a medium skillet with nonstick vegetable cooking spray and place over high heat. Add the meat and sauté for 5 minutes. Reduce the heat to medium and add the onions, celery, bell pepper, salt and red pepper; cook for 15 minutes, stirring often. Add the Worcestershire sauce and browning sauce and cook 10 minutes longer, stirring often.

Stir in the dissolved bouillon and cook for 5 minutes. Remove from the heat and stir in the marinated artichokes. Spray the inside of a 9-inch-square baking dish with nonstick vegetable cooking spray. Add *half* of the rice, *half* of the cheese and *half* of the meat mixture. Repeat the process with the remaining ingredients. Bake for 15 minutes.

PER SERVING	KCAL	FATgm	CHOLmg	SODmg
	316	3.2	101	411

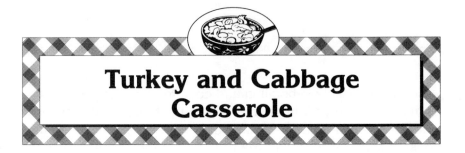

Turkey and Cabbage Casserole

F*or all you cabbage lovers, the mild, creamy taste of this dish will have you reaching for seconds . . . and thirds!*

MAKES 6 SERVINGS

1 cup finely chopped onions
½ cup finely chopped yellow bell pepper
½ cup finely chopped red bell pepper
1 pound ground turkey breast
½ teaspoon salt
½ teaspoon ground red pepper
¼ cup tomato paste

½ cup salt-free chicken broth
1½ cups uncooked quick-cooking (not instant) rice
4 cups shredded cabbage
Four ¾-ounce slices reduced-fat American cheese product, cut into thin strips

Preheat the oven to 400°F.

Spray the inside of a medium skillet with butter-flavored non-stick vegetable cooking spray and place over high heat. Add the onions and bell peppers and sauté for 5 minutes. Add the turkey, salt and red pepper; cook and stir for 10 minutes. Dissolve the tomato paste in the chicken broth and set aside.

Spray the inside of a 9-inch-square baking dish with butter-flavored nonstick vegetable cooking spray. Add the rice, then

layer with *half* of the cabbage and *half* of the meat mixture. Repeat the layers with the remaining cabbage and meat mixture. Pour in the dissolved tomato paste. Cover and bake for 45 minutes. Remove from the oven and top with the cheese. Return to the oven and bake 3 minutes longer, or until the cheese is melted.

PER SERVING	KCAL	FATgm	CHOLmg	SODmg
	299	3.6	63	504

Turkey-Mirliton Casserole

MAKES 6 SERVINGS

5 cups water
5 mirlitons (page xiv), cut
    in half
1 pound ground turkey
    breast
1 cup chopped onions
1/2 cup chopped green bell
    pepper
1/2 cup chopped red bell
    pepper
1/2 teaspoon browning and
    seasoning sauce
1/2 teaspoon salt
1/2 teaspoon ground red
    pepper

1 cup salt-free chicken
    broth
One 10 3/4-ounce can 99%
    fat-free cream of
    mushroom soup
1/4 cup finely chopped green
    onions
1 tablespoon very finely
    chopped fresh parsley
2 cups cooked rice
1/2 cup shredded reduced-fat
    Cheddar cheese

Preheat the oven to 350°F.

In a 5-quart Dutch oven over high heat, bring the water to a boil. Add the mirlitons and cook for 8 to 10 minutes, or until tender. Remove from the heat; place the mirlitons in ice water for 5 minutes to cool, then peel and seed. Coarsely chop the pulp and set aside.

Spray the inside of a heavy skillet with nonstick vegetable cooking spray and place over high heat. Add the meat and sauté for 10 minutes. Add the next 6 ingredients; cook and stir for 10 minutes. Stir in the broth and cook for 5 minutes. Add the soup,

green onions and parsley; cook, stirring, 5 minutes longer. Remove from the heat and add the cooked rice; mix well.

Spoon the mixture into a 9-inch-square baking dish that has been sprayed with nonstick vegetable cooking spray. Top with the cheese and bake for 20 minutes.

PER SERVING	KCAL	FATgm	CHOLmg	SODmg
	152	2	66	456

C.J.'s Enchilada Casserole

When C.J., my 12-month-old grandson, had a taste of this dish, he kept pointing to the stove for more. I also make this dish with chicken and it's just as good.

MAKES 8 SERVINGS

1 teaspoon salt
1 teaspoon ground white
  pepper
¼ teaspoon ground cumin
¼ teaspoon dried oregano
  leaves, crushed
1 pound beef flank steak,
  cut into ½-inch strips
1 cup finely chopped onions
½ cup finely chopped bell
  pepper

2 tablespoons chopped mild
  green chili pepper
1½ teaspoons chili powder
One 16-ounce can salt-free
  whole tomatoes,
  chopped
½ cup shredded reduced-fat
  Cheddar cheese
8 corn tortillas

Preheat the oven to 375°F.

Combine the salt, white pepper, cumin and oregano and sprinkle over the meat. Spray the inside of a large skillet with nonstick vegetable cooking spray and place over medium heat. Add the meat and sauté for 10 minutes, or until it is browned. Add the onions, bell pepper, chili pepper and chili powder; Cook and stir for 10 minutes. Add the tomatoes and cook 5 minutes longer. Add ¼ cup of the cheese; remove from heat and stir until the cheese is melted.

Spoon equal portions of the meat mixture into the middle of each tortilla; fold the tortillas in thirds across the filling and turn them seam side down. Place the tortillas in a baking dish that has been sprayed with nonstick vegetable cooking spray. Top with the remaining cheese and bake for 15 minutes.

PER SERVING	KCAL	FATgm	CHOLmg	SODmg
	228	7.9	53	368

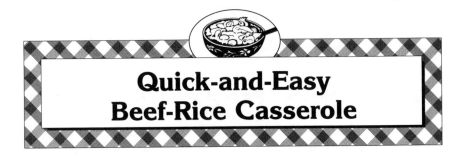

Quick-and-Easy
Beef-Rice Casserole

If you want a light and tasty lunch, try this dish. Serve alone or with Creamy Cauliflower (page 212).

MAKES 4 SERVINGS

½ pound beef flank steak, cut into 1-inch strips
¼ teaspoon salt
1 cup chopped onions
1 cup thinly sliced fresh mushrooms
½ cup chopped green bell pepper

½ cup chopped red bell pepper
1 tablespoon sliced jalapeño pepper
1 tablespoon salt-free beef bouillon granules
1½ cups water
2 cups quick-cooking rice

Preheat the oven to 350°F.

Sprinkle the meat with the salt. Spray the inside of a medium skillet with nonstick vegetable cooking spray and place over high heat. Add the meat and sauté for 5 minutes, or until browned on all sides. Add the onions, mushrooms, bell peppers and jalapeño; cook and stir for 5 minutes. Dissolve the bouillon granules in the water and add to the skillet, stirring well.

Put the rice in a baking dish and spoon the meat mixture on top. Cover and bake for 20 minutes.

PER SERVING	KCAL	FATgm	CHOLmg	SODmg
	252	6.8	52	240

Beef Stew, Prudhomme-Style

1 pound boneless beef
   steak, cut into bite-size
   pieces
5 cups water
3 carrots, chopped
2 cups peeled and cubed
   russet potatoes
1 cup chopped onions
1 cup Roux Flour (page
   289)
½ cup chopped celery

1 teaspoon salt
1 teaspoon dried basil
   leaves, crushed
½ teaspoon ground white
   pepper
¼ cup finely chopped green
   onions
2 tablespoons finely
   chopped fresh parsley
3 cups hot cooked rice

Spray the inside of a 5-quart Dutch oven with nonstick vegetable cooking spray and place over high heat. Add the meat and sauté for 10 minutes, or until browned. Add the next 9 ingredients. Reduce the heat to medium and cook for 15 minutes. Reduce the heat to a simmer; cover and cook for 20 minutes, or until the meat is tender. Remove from the heat; stir in the green onions and parsley and let stand for 5 minutes. Serve over rice.

PER SERVING	KCAL	FATgm	CHOLmg	SODmg
	366	9.3	87	475

Turkey Meatball Stew

I used ground turkey to make the meatballs for this dish, and it tastes great. It also cuts down on the fat grams.

MAKES 6 SERVINGS

1 pound ground turkey breast
1 small potato, peeled and grated
1 cup very finely chopped onions
⅓ cup very finely chopped green onions

2 tablespoons very finely chopped fresh parsley
2 teaspoons ground red pepper
1½ teaspoons salt
6 cups water
1 cup Roux Flour (page 289)
3 cups hot cooked rice

In a large bowl, combine the meat, potato, *half* of the onions, *half* of the green onions, *half* of the parsley, *half* of the red pepper and *½ teaspoon* of the salt. Mix well and shape into 12 meatballs.

In a 5-quart Dutch oven over high heat, bring the water to a boil. Stir in the roux flour. Reduce the heat to medium and add the meatballs, one at a time. Add all the remaining ingredients, stirring well. Cook for 20 minutes, stirring often. Remove from the heat and serve over rice.

PER SERVING	KCAL	FATgm	CHOLmg	SODmg
	194	0.9	63	538

PASTA

Spicy Turkey Sausage Rotini

This sumptuous dish is quick to prepare. Best of all, when you are all through, you have only one skillet to wash!

MAKES 4 SERVINGS

*½ pound Smoked Turkey
    Sausage (page 144),
    thinly sliced
½ cup finely chopped
    onions
½ cup finely chopped red
    bell pepper
One 10-ounce can reduced-
    calorie cream of
    mushroom soup*

*2 tablespoons chopped
    jalapeño pepper
3 cups cooked rotini
    (corkscrew-shaped
    pasta)
1 cup evaporated skim milk*

Spray the inside of a medium skillet with nonstick vegetable cooking spray and place over high heat. Add the turkey sausage, onions and bell pepper and sauté for 5 minutes. Reduce the heat to medium, add the mushroom soup and jalapeño, and cook for 5 minutes. Add the pasta and milk; cook, stirring, 8 minutes longer, or until the sauce thickens.

PER SERVING	KCAL	FATgm	CHOLmg	SODmg
	314	2	50	480

Rotini with Carrots and Basil

This dish can be served as a light lunch or as a side dish with meat, fish, or poultry. The fresh basil adds just the right touch.

MAKES 5 SERVINGS

1 tablespoon extra virgin olive oil
2 cups thinly sliced baby carrots
2 plum tomatoes, peeled, seeded and chopped
1/3 cup salt-free chicken broth
1 teaspoon minced fresh garlic

1/4 teaspoon salt
1/4 teaspoon ground black pepper
4 cups cooked rotini (corkscrew-shaped pasta)
2 tablespoons finely chopped fresh basil

Heat the oil in a medium skillet over high heat. Add the carrots and tomatoes; cook and stir for 3 minutes. Add the broth, garlic, salt and pepper; cook and stir for another 3 minutes. Add the pasta and basil; cook 5 minutes longer, stirring often.

PER SERVING	KCAL	FATgm	CHOLmg	SODmg
	220	3.9	0	144

Rotini with Canadian Bacon

If you can't find Anaheim peppers, substitute banana peppers or bell peppers. Whichever you choose, you definitely won't lose!

MAKES 4 SERVINGS

½ pound Canadian bacon
3 plum tomatoes, peeled, seeded and chopped
1 large roasted Anaheim chili pepper (page 220) chopped
¼ cup very finely chopped red bell pepper

1 cup salt-free chicken broth
1 teaspoon ground black pepper
3 cups cooked rotini (corkscrew-shaped pasta)
1 cup evaporated skim milk

Spray the inside of a large skillet with nonstick vegetable cooking spray and place over medium heat. Add the bacon and sauté for 3 minutes. Add the tomatoes, chili pepper and bell pepper; cook and stir for 5 minutes. Stir in the broth and black pepper and cook 5 minutes longer. Add the pasta and milk; cook, stirring, for 10 minutes, or until the sauce thickens.

PER SERVING	KCAL	FATgm	CHOLmg	SODmg
	314	5.9	35	956

Tuna and Bow-Tie Pasta

If you don't like canned tuna, substitute crabmeat. It's even better!

MAKES 4 SERVINGS

4 cups water
⅓ cup dehydrated onion
1 tablespoon salt-free
    chicken bouillon
    granules
3 cups uncooked bow-tie
    pasta
Two 6⅛-ounce cans tuna
    packed in water,
    drained

½ cup reduced-calorie
    mayonnaise
3 ounces reduced-fat
    process cheese spread,
    shredded
1 tablespoon salt-free
    lemon-pepper
    seasoning
1 tablespoon butter-flavored
    sprinkles

In a 5-quart Dutch oven over high heat, bring the water to a boil. Add the onion and bouillon granules and boil for 3 minutes. Add the pasta and cook for 10 minutes. Remove from the heat, drain the pasta, then place in a large bowl. Add the tuna, mayonnaise, cheese, lemon-pepper seasoning and butter-flavored granules and mix well.

PER SERVING	KCAL	FATgm	CHOLmg	SODmg
	346	6.3	58	690

Southern Fettuccine Alfredo

There are lots of ways to make alfredo sauce. Try this version—it's very tasty!

MAKES 2 SERVINGS

1 cup skim milk
¼ cup finely chopped green
onions
½ teaspoon olive oil
⅛ teaspoon salt
⅛ teaspoon ground black
pepper

1 tablespoon chopped
pimiento
1 tablespoon freshly grated
Parmesan cheese
2 cups cooked fettuccine

In a medium skillet over high heat, combine the milk, green onions, olive oil, salt and pepper. Cook and stir for 5 minutes. Add the pimiento and cheese; stir until the cheese is melted. Remove from the heat and add the fettuccine; toss well and serve immediately.

PER SERVING	KCAL	FATgm	CHOLmg	SODmg
	265	3.4	4	246

Tomato-Cheese Fettuccine

This dish is a favorite with our vegetarian customers. You can add sliced zucchini and yellow squash for variety.

MAKES 4 SERVINGS

One 10-ounce can whole
    tomatoes with chilies,
    chopped
2 tablespoons reduced-
    calorie margarine
1 tablespoon all-purpose
    flour
½ cup evaporated skim
    milk

Two ¾-ounce slices
    reduced-fat American
    cheese product
1 cup Buttermilk Salad
    Dressing (page 30)
3 cups cooked fettuccine

In a medium skillet over high heat, cook and stir the tomatoes for 2 minutes, or until reduced to about 2 tablespoons. Remove from the heat and set aside.

In a large skillet over low heat, melt the margarine. Add the flour; cook and stir about 1 minute, but do not let the flour brown. Stir in the milk and cook for 1 minute. Add the cheese, stirring constantly until it is melted. Add the buttermilk mixture, fettuccine and the reserved tomato. Cook for 5 minutes, stirring often.

PER SERVING	KCAL	FATgm	CHOLmg	SODmg
	250	6	1	450

Linguine with Sun-Dried Tomatoes and Basil

The sun-dried tomatoes give this dish a special flavor. You can find them in any major supermarket.

MAKES 4 SERVINGS

½ ounce sun-dried
   tomatoes
One 13¾-ounce can salt-
   free chicken broth
¼ teaspoon dried basil
   leaves, crushed
1 cup broccoli florets

2 tablespoons very finely
   chopped green onion
1 tablespoon very finely
   chopped fresh parsley
2 cups cooked linguine
½ teaspoon salt

Soak the tomatoes in *half* of the broth for 2 hours. In a medium saucepan over high heat, bring the remaining broth to a boil. Reduce the heat to medium and cook until the broth is reduced by half. Add the tomatoes with their broth and the basil; cook for 5 minutes. Add the broccoli, green onion and parsley, stirring well. Add the linguine and salt; cook and stir 5 minutes longer.

PER SERVING	KCAL	FATgm	CHOLmg	SODmg
	102	0.6	0	252

Linguine with Tuna

The original version of this dish was such a big hit at my restaurant, I decided to create this low-fat recipe for the book. You'll be amazed at the taste!

MAKES **6** SERVINGS

1 teaspoon paprika
½ teaspoon salt
½ teaspoon sugar
½ teaspoon granulated
 garlic
½ teaspoon onion powder
½ teaspoon ground thyme
½ teaspoon ground red
 pepper
½ teaspoon ground black
 pepper
1 pound fresh tuna fillets,
 cut ¾ inch thick
1 tablespoon reduced-
 calorie margarine

½ cup finely chopped
 onions
1 tablespoon all-purpose
 flour
One-half 10-ounce can
 cream of mushroom
 soup
1 cup salt-free chicken
 broth
3 tablespoons finely
 chopped green onion
3 tablespoons finely
 chopped fresh parsley
3 cups cooked linguine
1 cup evaporated skim milk

Preheat a charcoal or gas grill.

Combine the first 8 ingredients in a small bowl. Mix well and reserve *1 teaspoon* for later use. Sprinkle the remaining seasoning mix over both sides of the fish. Place the fish on the hot grill and cook for 4 minutes on each side, or until it flakes easily with a fork. Remove from the heat; set aside and keep warm.

Melt the margarine in a medium skillet over high heat. Add the onions and sauté for 3 minutes. Add the flour; cook and stir for 3 minutes. Add the mushroom soup, broth, green onion, parsley and reserved seasoning mix. Cook and stir for 5 minutes. Add the milk and pasta; cook 5 minutes longer or until the sauce thickens.

Remove the pasta and sauce to a plate. Place the tuna over the pasta and serve.

PER SERVING	KCAL	FATgm	CHOLmg	SODmg
	217	2.3	36	264

Angelhair Pasta with Turkey Sausage, Tomato and Basil

This is a delicious main dish that can be prepared in about 28 minutes.

MAKES 4 SERVINGS

1 pound smoked Turkey
    Sausage (page 144),
    cut into bite-size pieces
1 cup finely chopped onions
1 cup thinly sliced
    mushrooms
1½ cups salt-free chicken
    broth
1 cup stewed tomatoes

1 dried hot chili pepper,
    crushed
2 tablespoons finely
    chopped green onion
¼ teaspoon dried basil
    leaves, crushed
2 cups cooked angelhair
    pasta

Spray the inside of a medium skillet with nonstick vegetable cooking spray and place over high heat. Add the sausage, onions and mushrooms and sauté for 3 minutes. Add the broth and to-matoes; cook and stir for 10 minutes. Reduce the heat to me-dium, cover, and cook for 10 minutes. Add the chili pepper, green onion and basil; cook and stir for 5 minutes. Add the pasta and cook 5 minutes longer. Remove from the heat and let stand for 5 minutes before serving.

PER SERVING	KCAL	FATgm	CHOLmg	SODmg
	304	1.8	95	225

Vermicelli with Fresh Tomato Sauce

A *hearty main dish that's as easy to prepare as 1-2-3!*

MAKES 4 SERVINGS

1 tablespoon olive oil
4 plum tomatoes, peeled,
*   seeded and chopped*
1 teaspoon minced fresh
*   garlic*

1 teaspoon dried basil
*   leaves, crushed*
2 cups cooked vermicelli
1 tablespoon grated
*   Parmesan cheese*

Heat the oil in a medium skillet over high heat. When very hot, add the tomatoes, garlic and basil; cook and stir for 10 minutes. Add the vermicelli, stirring well. Remove from the heat and place on a warm plate. Sprinkle with the cheese.

PER SERVING	KCAL	FATgm	CHOLmg	SODmg
	137	4.7	3	28

Brett's Chicken Spaghetti

My great-grandson Brett's favorite dish. All your grandchildren and children will love it.

MAKES 6 SERVINGS

1 cup chopped yellow
    onions
1 cup chopped red onions
1 cup chopped bell pepper
1 pound skinned and boned
    chicken breast, cut into
    ½-inch cubes
1 teaspoon salt
1 teaspoon ground white
    pepper

1 teaspoon dried basil
    leaves, crushed
One 16-ounce can salt-free
    whole tomatoes
One 13¾-ounce can salt-
    free chicken broth
3 tablespoons tomato paste
6 cups hot cooked spaghetti

Spray the inside of a 5-quart Dutch oven with butter-flavored nonstick vegetable cooking spray and place over high heat. Add the onions and bell pepper and sauté for 5 minutes. Spray the pot again with cooking spray and add the chicken, salt, white pepper and basil. Cook for 10 minutes, stirring often. Add the tomatoes, broth and tomato paste and reduce the heat to medium. Cover and cook for 20 minutes, stirring often. Add the spaghetti and stir well. Remove from the heat and let stand for 10 minutes before serving.

PER SERVING	KCAL	FATgm	CHOLmg	SODmg
	162	3.3	65	388

Oven-Baked Macaroni and Cheese

MAKES 4 SERVINGS

2 cups cooked macaroni
1 tablespoon very finely
  chopped onion
1 teaspoon sugar
1/4 teaspoon salt
1/8 teaspoon ground white
  pepper

1 egg
1 cup evaporated skim milk
1/2 cup shredded reduced-fat
  Cheddar cheese

Preheat the oven to 350°F.

In a medium bowl, stir together the macaroni, onion, sugar, salt and pepper. Beat the egg with the milk and gradually stir into the macaroni mixture; add the cheese and mix well.

Spray the inside of a 4-quart casserole dish with nonstick vegetable cooking spray. Spoon the macaroni mixture into the dish and bake for 30 minutes.

PER SERVING	KCAL	FATgm	CHOLmg	SODmg
	198	4.3	78	257

Stuffed Jumbo Shells with Tomato Sauce

When *my son-in-law tried this dish, he liked it so much that he went home and made it for dinner!*

MAKES 4 SERVINGS

5 quarts water
16 jumbo pasta shells
1 pound ground turkey
    breast
½ teaspoon salt
¼ teaspoon dried basil
    leaves, crushed
¼ teaspoon dried oregano
    leaves, crushed
¼ cup shredded reduced-fat
    Cheddar cheese
1 cup finely chopped onions

½ cup finely chopped bell
    pepper
One 16-ounce can salt-free
    whole tomatoes,
    chopped
One 13¾-ounce can salt-
    free chicken broth
3 tablespoons finely
    chopped green onion
2 tablespoons finely
    chopped fresh parsley

In a large stockpot over high heat, bring the water to a boil. Add the pasta shells and cook for 15 minutes. Remove from the heat, drain, rinse under cold water and set aside. Spray the inside of a 5-quart Dutch oven with nonstick vegetable cooking spray and place over high heat. Add the meat, ¼ *teaspoon* of the salt, the basil and oregano and cook for 5 minutes, stirring often. Remove from the heat and stir in the cheese. Let cool to the touch. Fill each pasta shell with 2 teaspoons of the meat mixture; set aside.

Spray the same pot again with the cooking spray and place over high heat. Add the onions and bell pepper and sauté for 5

minutes. Stir in the tomatoes and broth and cook for 10 minutes, stirring often.

Carefully put the stuffed shells in the pot. Reduce the heat to medium, cover, and cook for 20 minutes, stirring occasionally. Stir in the green onion and parsley. Remove from the heat and let stand, covered, for 10 minutes before serving.

PER SERVING	KCAL	FATgm	CHOLmg	SODmg
	196	2.3	100	394

Chicken Lasagna

MAKES 8 SERVINGS

6 lasagna noodles
6 cups water
One 2½-pound chicken,
    skin and fat removed
1 tablespoon olive oil
2 cups chopped onions
¼ cup tomato paste
2 teaspoons minced fresh
    garlic

1½ teaspoons salt
1 teaspoon fennel seed
½ teaspoon dried oregano
    leaves, crushed
1 cup fat-free ricotta cheese
1 cup shredded reduced-fat
    Cheddar-Jack cheese

Cook the lasagna noodles according to package directions, omitting the salt; drain and set aside. In a 5-quart Dutch oven over high heat, bring the water to a boil. Add the chicken and cook, covered, for 15 minutes. Remove from heat; drain the chicken and reserve 2 cups of the stock for later use. Let the chicken cool to the touch, then debone it and shred the meat; set aside.

Preheat the oven to 375°F.

In a medium skillet over high heat, heat the oil. When very hot, add the onions and sauté for 5 minutes. Dissolve the tomato paste in the reserved stock and add to the skillet along with the garlic, salt, fennel seed and oregano; cook for 15 minutes, stirring often. Add the shredded chicken and cook 5 minutes longer. Remove from the heat.

Spray the inside of a 9-by-12-inch baking dish with butter-flavored nonstick vegetable cooking spray. Place *half* of the lasagna noodles in the dish, add *half* of the meat mixture, *half* of the ricotta and *half* of the Cheddar-Jack cheese. Repeat the process until all the ingredients are used. Cover and bake for 20 minutes. Uncover and bake 15 minutes longer.

PER SERVING	KCAL	FATgm	CHOLmg	SODmg
	279	9.8	99	480

Vegetable Lasagna

1½ teaspoons garlic powder
1 teaspoon salt
½ teaspoon fennel seed
½ teaspoon dried oregano leaves, crushed
½ teaspoon dried basil leaves, crushed
½ teaspoon ground red pepper
One 6-ounce can tomato paste
½ cup salt-free chicken broth

12 cooked lasagna noodles
3 tomatoes, peeled, seeded and chopped
2 cups thinly sliced yellow squash
2 cups thinly sliced zucchini
1 cup finely chopped onions
1 cup cauliflowerettes
1 cup shredded reduced-fat Cheddar cheese
½ cup chopped yellow bell pepper

Preheat the oven to 450 degrees.

In a small bowl, combine the first 6 ingredients; mix well and set aside. Dissolve the tomato paste in the broth and set aside. Place *6* lasagna noodles in a 9-inch-square baking dish that has been sprayed with nonstick vegetable cooking spray. Add *half* of the tomatoes, *half* of the yellow squash, *half* of the zucchini, *half* of the onions, *half* of the cauliflower, *half* of the dissolved tomato paste and *half* of the shredded cheese half of the bell pepper. Repeat the process, ending with the cheese. Cover and bake for 1 hour.

PER SERVING	KCAL	FATgm	CHOLmg	SODmg
	78	1.4	3.8	415

Lemon-Parmesan Pasta Salad

To make this a warm salad, combine the ingredients soon after the pasta is cooked and serve. For a cold salad, rinse the fettuccine in cold water after cooking and chill the salad after mixing (or use cold leftover pasta).

MAKES 3 SERVINGS

3 cups cooked fettuccine
⅓ cup Lemon-Parmesan
    Dressing (page 32)
1 tablespoon very finely
    chopped green onion

1 teaspoon chopped
    pimiento
1 teaspoon minced fresh
    parsley

Combine all the ingredients in a bowl and mix well.

PER SERVING	KCAL	FATgm	CHOLmg	SODmg
	210	2	3	31

RICE, DRESSINGS AND OTHER SIDE DISHES

Basic White Rice

2 cups water   *2 cups converted rice*

Combine the water and rice in a 2-quart saucepan. Cover and bring to a boil over medium heat; cook for 10 minutes. Reduce the heat to a simmer; simmer 5 minutes longer. Serve hot.

PER ½-CUP SERVING	KCAL	FATgm	CHOLmg	SODmg
	171	0.3	0	1

Vegetarian Rice

This is a hearty main meal vegetarians will love. It's also a great side dish with meat, fish or poultry. Try it!

MAKES 4 SERVINGS

1 teaspoon vegetable-
flavored salt-free
bouillon granules
1½ cups water
1 cup converted rice
1 carrot, thinly sliced
¼ cup finely chopped onion
1 small zucchini, cut into
½-inch cubes

1 cup broccoli florets
¼ cup finely chopped red
bell pepper
1 tablespoon salt-free
lemon-pepper
seasoning

In a medium saucepan, dissolve the bouillon granules in the water, then place over medium heat. Add the rice and bring to a boil. Reduce the heat to a simmer, cover and cook for 5 minutes, stirring often. Remove from the heat and keep warm.

Spray the inside of a large skillet with butter-flavored nonstick vegetable cooking spray and place over medium heat. Add the carrot and onion and sauté for 3 minutes. Add the zucchini, broccoli, bell pepper and lemon-pepper seasoning; cook and stir for 10 minutes. Add the rice with bouillon. Reduce the heat to a simmer, cover and cook for 10 minutes, or until the rice is tender.

PER SERVING	KCAL	FATgm	CHOLmg	SODmg
	193	0.5	0	18

270

Spanish Rice

This is a great side dish. Serve with meat, fish or poultry or with any of the enchilada recipes in this book.

MAKES 4 SERVINGS

1 cup chopped onions
2 tablespoons salt-free beef bouillon granules
2 cups water
One 10½-ounce can tomatoes with green chilies
1 tomato, peeled, seeded and chopped

2 tablespoons tomato paste
1 teaspoon salt
1 bay leaf
1 cup converted rice
¼ cup finely chopped green onions

Spray the inside of a 5-quart Dutch oven with nonstick vegetable cooking spray and place over high heat. Add the onions and sauté for 5 minutes. Dissolve the bouillon granules in the water and add to the pot along with the next 5 ingredients. Cook for 10 minutes, stirring often. Reduce the heat to medium; add the rice and cook, covered, for 10 minutes, or until the rice is tender. Remove from the heat and stir in the green onions. Let stand, covered, for 5 minutes. Remove the bay leaf before serving.

PER SERVINGS	KCAL	FATgm	CHOLmg	SODmg
	201	0.5	0	704

Baked Texas Rice

I *serve this rice dish to guests with a grilled chicken breast and fresh vegetables.*

MAKES 6 SERVINGS

1 cup low-fat cottage cheese
3 tablespoons evaporated skim milk
1 tablespoon lemon juice
1 cup very finely chopped onions
½ cup very finely chopped celery
½ cup very finely chopped green bell pepper
½ cup very finely chopped red bell pepper

1 tablespoon salt-free chicken bouillon granules
1¼ cups water
One 3½-ounce can sliced jalapeño peppers
¼ teaspoon salt
2 cups uncooked quick-cooking rice
½ cup shredded reduced-fat Cheddar cheese

Preheat the oven to 375°F.

Place the cottage cheese, milk and lemon juice in a blender and process until smooth; set aside.

Spray the inside of a medium skillet with butter-flavored non-stick vegetable cooking spray and place over high heat. Add the onions, celery and bell peppers; reduce the heat to medium and cook for 5 minutes, stirring constantly. Dissolve the bouillon granules in the water and add to the skillet. Cook and stir for 5 minutes. Add the blended cottage cheese and cook for 2 minutes.

Reduce the heat to a simmer; add the jalapeños and salt and cook 5 minutes longer, stirring often.

Put the rice in a 9-inch-square baking dish. Spoon the mixture over the rice and top with the cheese. Cover and bake for 20 minutes.

PER SERVING	KCAL	FATgm	CHOLmg	SODmg
	110	0.6	2	426

Taco Rice

Simply delicious, this recipe can be used as a side dish to almost everything.

MAKES 8 SERVINGS

1 cup finely chopped onions
½ green bell pepper, thinly
    sliced
½ red bell pepper, thinly
    sliced
One 16-ounce can salt-free
    whole tomatoes

3 cups salt-free chicken
    broth
1 package taco seasoning
    mix
2 cups converted rice
½ teaspoon salt (optional)

Spray the inside of a 5-quart Dutch oven with nonstick vegetable cooking spray and place over high heat. Add the onions, bell peppers and tomatoes and cook for 5 minutes, stirring often and mashing the tomatoes with a spoon. Stir in the broth and taco mix and bring to a boil. Add the rice and salt; reduce the heat to a simmer and cook, covered, for 20 minutes, stirring occasionally.

PER SERVING	KCAL	FATgm	CHOLmg	SODmg
	72	0.2	0	124

Eggplant Rice Dressing

MAKES 5 SERVINGS

2 cups water
1 medium eggplant, peeled
  and diced (about 2
  cups)
1 pound ground turkey
  breast
1 cup chopped onions
½ cup chopped green bell
  pepper
½ cup chopped red bell
  pepper

½ teaspoon salt
½ teaspoon ground white
  pepper
½ teaspoon paprika
1 tablespoon salt-free
  chicken bouillon
  granules
2 cups cooked rice
2 tablespoons finely
  chopped green onion

In a medium saucepan, bring *1 cup* of the water to a boil over high heat. Add the eggplant and cook, covered, for 5 minutes. Remove from heat, drain and set aside.

Spray the inside of a large skillet with butter-flavored nonstick vegetable cooking spray and place over high heat. Add the turkey and sauté for 5 minutes. Add the next 6 ingredients, reduce the heat to medium and cook for 10 minutes, stirring often. Dissolve the bouillon granules in the remaining 1 cup water and add to the skillet. Increase the heat to high and cook, stirring, for 10 minutes. Add the eggplant; cook and stir for 10 minutes. Add the rice and green onion and mix well. Remove from the heat and let stand for 5 minutes before serving.

PER SERVING	KCAL	FATgm	CHOLmg	SODmg
	226	1	76	249

DIPS, SALSAS AND SAUCES

Vegetable Dip

This dip is light and creamy. Serve with crackers or raw vegetables at your next party.

MAKES 1 CUP

One 3-ounce package
reduced-calorie soft
cream cheese
¼ cup reduced-calorie
mayonnaise
¼ cup evaporated skim
milk
¼ cup very finely chopped
onion
¼ cup finely chopped dill
pickle

2 tablespoons finely
chopped fresh parsley
½ teaspoon garlic powder
⅛ teaspoon salt
⅛ teaspoon paprika
⅛ teaspoon ground red
pepper
⅛ teaspoon ground black
pepper

In a medium bowl, combine the cream cheese and mayonnaise and beat with an electric mixer on low speed until smooth. Add all the remaining ingredients and beat 5 minutes longer, or until well mixed.

PER TABLESPOON	KCAL	FATgm	CHOLmg	SODmg
	32	2.2	6	82

Shrimp and Jalapeño Dip

This dip will be a big hit at your next get-together. The perfect blend of shrimp and jalapeños makes your mouth think there's a party going on!

MAKES 1½ CUPS

1 cup low-fat cottage cheese
2 cups water
1 cup peeled and deveined
    small shrimp
⅓ cup reduced-calorie
    mayonnaise
8 pimiento-stuffed olives,
    finely chopped

1 tablespoon very finely
    chopped celery
1 tablespoon dehydrated
    onion
1 jalapeño pepper, finely
    chopped

Place the cottage cheese in a blender and process until smooth; set aside.

In a small saucepan over high heat, bring the water to a boil. Add the shrimp and cook for 5 minutes, or until pink. Drain and chop fine; set aside.

In a medium bowl, combine the mayonnaise, olives, celery, onion, jalapeño pepper and ⅓ cup of the blended cottage cheese. (Refrigerate the remaining cottage cheese for another use.) Stir until well mixed and refrigerate at least 1 hour before serving.

PER TABLESPOON	KCAL	FATgm	CHOLmg	SODmg
	16	1.1	8	49

Cucumber and Tomato Salsa

*T*ry *either with low-sodium chips, over chicken or on fish.*

1 cup vegetable juice
   cocktail
½ cup finely chopped
   onions
½ cup finely chopped celery
½ cup finely chopped green
   bell pepper
1 large tomato, peeled,
   seeded and chopped

1 small cucumber, peeled
   and diced
One 4-ounce can chopped
   green chili peppers
1 tablespoon lemon juice
¼ teaspoon salt

In a small saucepan over high heat, boil the vegetable juice for 8 to 10 minutes, or until reduced by half, stirring often. Remove from the heat and set aside.

Spray the inside of a medium skillet with nonstick vegetable cooking spray and place over high heat. Add the onions, celery and bell pepper and sauté for 5 minutes. Add the tomato, cucumber, chili peppers and reserved vegetable juice. Cook and stir for 5 minutes. Stir in the lemon juice and salt. Remove from the heat and let stand for 5 minutes before serving.

PER SERVINGS	KCAL	FATgm	CHOLmg	SODmg
	65	0.4	0	207

Corn Salsa

Serve over fish or poultry or with low-fat chips.

This recipe calls for a tomatillo, which is a vegetable that resembles a small green tomato. Available fresh and canned, tomatillos are used frequently in Mexican cooking. Anaheim peppers are long, thin, pale green chilies with a mild flavor; you can substitute poblanos. Serrano peppers are small, bright green, very hot chilies.

MAKES 1½ CUPS

3 tomatoes, peeled and seeded

1 tomatillo, peeled, seeded and chopped

½ cup whole-kernel corn, drained

⅛ cup very finely chopped red onion

2 tablespoons minced fresh Anaheim pepper

2 tablespoons minced fresh serrano pepper

1 tablespoon balsamic vinegar

½ teaspoon minced fresh garlic

¼ teaspoon salt

Place 2 of the tomatoes in a food processor and puree; chop the remaining tomato. Mix the tomatoes with all the remaining ingredients in a medium bowl. Cover with plastic wrap and refrigerate for 1 hour before serving.

PER TABLESPOON	KCAL	FATgm	CHOLmg	SODmg
	8	0.1	0	32

Taco Salsa

I *use fresh garden tomatoes in this recipe, but if they're not available in your area you can substitute canned stewed tomatoes. Everyone in the restaurant loves this dish!*

MAKES 1 CUP

1 large tomato, peeled,
    seeded and chopped
1 hot green chili pepper,
    chopped
3 tablespoons very finely
    chopped onion
1 tablespoon minced fresh
    garlic
1 teaspoon salt-free lemon-
    pepper seasoning
¼ teaspoon salt

¼ teaspoon dried basil
    leaves, crushed
⅛ teaspoon dried oregano
    leaves, crushed
1 small jalapeño pepper,
    very finely chopped
    (optional)
2 tablespoons very finely
    chopped green onion
1 tablespoon very finely
    chopped fresh parsley

Combine the first 8 ingredients in a large glass bowl and mix well. Stir in the jalapeño, green onion and parsley; let stand for 10 minutes before serving.

PER TABLESPOON	KCAL	FATgm	CHOLmg	SODmg
	6	0	0	35

Mustard Sauce

This sauce is superb over steamed vegetables or a baked potato.

MAKES 1½ CUPS

1 tablespoon reduced-
    calorie margarine
1½ cups evaporated skim
    milk
2 tablespoons Dijon
    mustard

1 teaspoon salt
1 teaspoon sugar
½ teaspoon ground white
    pepper
1 egg yolk
1 tablespoon cornstarch

Melt the margarine in a medium skillet over medium heat. Stir in
1 cup of the milk, the mustard, salt, sugar and white pepper. Cook
and stir for 3 minutes; remove from the heat. Beat the egg yolk
and cornstarch in the remaining ½ cup milk; gradually stir into
the skillet. Return the skillet to medium heat; cook and stir for 1
minute, but do not boil.

PER TABLESPOON	KCAL	FATgm	CHOLmg	SODmg
	21	0.5	12	122

Guacamole Sauce

Finally, you can enjoy the great taste of guacamole without all the fat. For variety, you can substitute sweet peas for the green beans and achieve the same results. Either way, you'll have a hard time convincing anyone that it's low-fat!

MAKES 1 CUP

*One 8-ounce can French-
style cut green beans,
drained*

*1 small avocado
¼ cup lemon juice*

Place the green beans in a food processor and process until smooth. Mash the avocado with a fork and stir in the lemon juice. Add the green bean puree and mix well.

PER TABLESPOON	KCAL	FATgm	CHOLmg	SODmg
	25	1.7	0	37

Cheese Sauce

This cheese sauce is easy to prepare and versatile.

MAKES ABOUT FOUR ¾-CUP SERVINGS

1 tablespoon reduced-
    calorie margarine
1 tablespoon all-purpose
    flour
½ cup evaporated skim
    milk

Two ¾-ounce slices
    reduced-fat American
    cheese product
½ teaspoon ground white
    pepper

Melt the margarine in a small skillet over low heat. Add the flour; cook and stir for a few seconds, being careful not to let the flour brown. Add the milk, cheese and pepper; stir until the cheese is melted and the sauce thickens.

PER SERVING	KCAL	FATgm	CHOLmg	SODmg
	79	3.5	1	281

Curry Sauce

MAKES 1 CUP

1 teaspoon cornstarch
⅛ teaspoon curry powder
1 cup evaporated skim milk

1 tablespoon very finely
chopped fresh parsley

Dissolve the cornstarch and curry powder in the milk. Spray the inside of a small skillet with nonstick vegetable cooking spray and place over high heat. Add the dissolved cornstarch mixture and bring to a boil. Reduce the heat to medium. Using a wire whisk, beat for 3 minutes, or until smooth and creamy. Add the parsley and cook 1 minute longer.

PER TABLESPOON	KCAL	FATgm	CHOLmg	SODmg
	13	0	1	18

Meat Loaf Sauce

I created this sauce to be served over meat loaf but later discovered that it works well with grilled chicken or fish.

MAKES 4 SERVINGS

*1 teaspoon reduced-calorie
 margarine*
*2 cups thinly sliced fresh
 mushrooms*
1 cup skim milk
*1 ounce reduced-fat
 processed cheese
 spread*

*1 tablespoon dehydrated
 onion*
*⅛ teaspoon ground black
 pepper*

Melt the margarine in a small saucepan over high heat. Add the mushrooms and cook for 2 minutes, stirring constantly. Add the remaining ingredients; cook and stir 2 minutes longer, or until the sauce thickens. Spoon the sauce over meat loaf.

PER SERVING	KCAL	FATgm	CHOLmg	SODmg
	53	1.8	5	157

Roux Flour

T raditionally, a roux is made from flour and fat, but who can afford all those extra calories? A roux lends taste and texture to many Cajun dishes, so I've developed one that is made by simply browning the flour, which adds the same flavor as a fat-based roux.

Roux flour is used in recipes throughout the book. It's not hard to make but, like a traditional roux, does require your full attention—so no phone calls or interruptions when making this recipe! If stored in a tightly covered container, roux flour will keep for 2 to 3 months.

Makes 4 cups

4 cups all-purpose flour

Place the flour in a large skillet over high heat; with a wire whisk, stir constantly for 25 minutes, or until the flour turns the color of light brown sugar. If the flour begins to darken too fast, remove the skillet from the heat and stir to allow the flour to cool and color evenly, then put it back on a lower heat setting. When the flour is browned, remove from the heat and continue stirring until it is completely cooled. Sift the flour into a container and store, covered, until needed.

PER CUP	KCAL	FATgm	CHOLmg	SODmg
	340	1	0	0

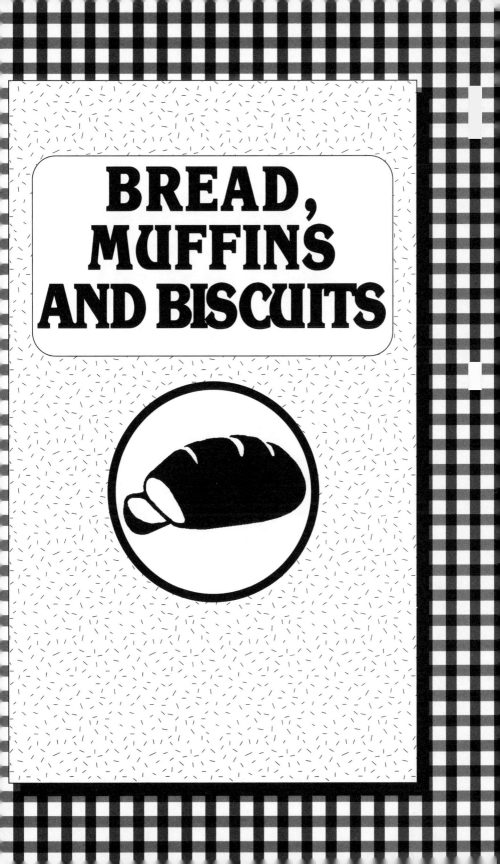

BREAD, MUFFINS AND BISCUITS

Three-Pepper Bread

*T*his bread is delicious. Don't let the name fool you—it's not real spicy, just plain good!

MAKES FOUR ½-POUND LOAVES

1¼ cups hot water
¼ cup nonfat dry milk
One ¼-ounce packet dry
    yeast
3 tablespoons sugar
1 teaspoon salt
3 dried mild chili peppers,
    crushed

¼ cup egg substitute
3 tablespoons reduced-
    calorie margarine
1 teaspoon ground white
    pepper
1 teaspoon ground black
    pepper
3½ cups bread flour

In a medium bowl, combine the water, milk, yeast, sugar and salt and stir well. Add the chili peppers, egg substitute, margarine, white pepper and black pepper, stirring well. Stir in the flour, 1 cup at a time, mixing well. With floured hands, place the dough on a lightly floured surface and knead until it is smooth and slightly sticky to the touch. Place the dough in a large bowl that has been sprayed with nonstick vegetable cooking spray. Spray the top of the dough with the cooking spray and cover with a clean, dry towel; let stand in a warm place until doubled in size.

Remove the towel and, with your fist, punch the dough down, then place it on a lightly floured surface. Divide the dough into 4 equal pieces. Shape each piece into a loaf by pressing down and rolling with the palm of your hand and your fingertips, tucking in the sides while rolling.

Spray four 2-by-6-by-3-inch loaf pans with nonstick vegetable cooking spray. Put the dough in the pans and cover with a dry towel; allow the dough to rise until it doubles in size again. Meanwhile, preheat the oven to 350°F. Remove the towel and bake the bread for 30 minutes, or until golden brown on top. Let the bread cool for 10 minutes before serving.

PER LOAF	KCAL	FATgm	CHOLmg	SODmg
	395	5.4	1	624

Blake's Chocolate Bread

MAKES FOUR ½-POUND LOAVES

1 cup warm skim milk
One ¼-ounce packet dry
    yeast
½ cup sugar
¼ teaspoon salt
2 ounces unsweetened
    chocolate, melted
1 egg, beaten
3 tablespoons reduced-
    calorie margarine

3 tablespoons unsweetened
    cocoa
1 teaspoon chocolate-
    flavored extract
½ teaspoon almond-
    flavored extract
½ teaspoon imitation butter
    flavoring
3 cups bread flour

In a medium bowl, combine the milk, yeast, sugar and salt; stir well and let stand for 5 minutes. Add all the remaining ingredients *except* the flour, stirring well. Gradually stir in the flour, mixing well. With floured hands, place the dough on a lightly floured surface and knead until it is smooth and slightly sticky to the touch.

Place the dough in a large bowl that has been sprayed with nonstick vegetable cooking spray. Spray the top of the dough with the cooking spray and cover with a clean, dry towel; let stand in a warm place until doubled in size.

Remove the towel and, with your fist, punch the dough down, then place it on a lightly floured surface. Divide the dough into 4 equal pieces. Shape each piece into a loaf by pressing down and rolling with the palm of your hand and your fingertips, tucking in the sides while rolling.

Spray four 2-by-6-by-3-inch loaf pans with nonstick vegetable cooking spray. Put the dough in pans and cover with a dry towel; allow the dough to rise until it doubles in size again. Meanwhile, preheat the oven to 350°F. Remove the towel and bake the bread for 35 minutes. Let the bread cool for 15 minutes before serving.

PER LOAF	KCAL	FATgm	CHOLmg	SODmg
	228	3.3	36	97

Plain Muffins

This recipe is so easy to prepare, even the kids will enjoy making it.

MAKES 12 MUFFINS

2 cups all-purpose flour
3 tablespoons sugar
1 tablespoon baking powder
1 teaspoon baking soda
½ teaspoon salt

Pinch of ground nutmeg
1 cup evaporated skim milk
2 tablespoons vegetable
   shortening
1 egg, beaten

Preheat the oven to 425°F.

In a medium bowl, sift together the flour, sugar, baking powder, baking soda and salt. Add the remaining ingredients and stir just until the dry ingredients are moistened. Spoon the batter into a muffin pan that has been sprayed with nonstick vegetable cooking spray. Bake for 20 minutes, or until the muffins start to brown.

PER MUFFIN	KCAL	FATgm	CHOLmg	SODmg
	111	2.8	24	265

Granola Biscuits

Serve these biscuits for breakfast or brunch. Everyone will love them.

Makes 18 Biscuits

3 egg whites
1 egg
1 teaspoon brown sugar
   substitute
⅛ cup reduced-calorie
   margarine
2 cups all-purpose flour
1 can evaporated skim milk

½ teaspoon baking powder
½ teaspoon imitation
   vanilla butter-nut
   flavoring
¼ teaspoon baking soda
¼ teaspoon salt
1½ cups dry granola cereal

Preheat the oven to 375°F.

In a large bowl, combine egg whites, egg, brown sugar substitute and margarine. Beat with an electric mixer on high speed for 1 minute, or until the mixture turns light yellow. Add the next 6 ingredients and mix well. Stir in the granola.

Spray a baking sheet with nonstick vegetable cooking spray. Using a small ice cream scoop, drop scoops of dough onto the baking sheet about 1 inch apart. Bake for 15 minutes, or until the biscuits are lightly browned.

PER BISCUIT	KCAL	FATgm	CHOLmg	SODmg
	108	2.7	16	117

DESSERTS

Banana Crunch

This low-fat dessert is easy to prepare and tastes so rich that no one will believe it's not fattening!

MAKES 4 SERVINGS

4 bananas
⅓ cup evaporated skim
    milk
¼ cup reduced-calorie soft-
    style cream cheese
One-half 10-ounce jar
    apricot fruit spread
½ teaspoon imitation butter
    flavoring

⅛ teaspoon ground
    cinnamon
⅛ teaspoon ground nutmeg
8 miniature apple-
    cinnamon-flavored rice
    cakes, crushed
2 tablespoons very finely
    chopped pecans

Peel the bananas and slice in half lengthwise; set aside. Combine the next 6 ingredients in a medium skillet over medium heat and bring to a boil. Reduce the heat to a simmer; add the bananas and cook for 3 minutes, stirring often. Remove from the heat and place on 4 warm plates. Top with crushed rice cakes and pecans. Serve warm.

PER SERVING	KCAL	FATgm	CHOLmg	SODmg
	288	3.4	1	26

Ambrosia

2 navel oranges, peeled and
   sectioned
1 apple, peeled and chopped
1 banana, peeled and thinly
   sliced
One 8-ounce can sliced
   peaches, drained
One 8-ounce can
   unsweetened pineapple
   chunks, drained

2 tablespoons shredded
   coconut
½ teaspoon liquid sugar
   substitute
½ cup frozen reduced-
   calorie whipped
   topping, thawed

Combine all the ingredients *except* the whipped topping in a large
bowl and mix well. Carefully fold in the whipped topping. Refrigerate for 1 hour before serving.

PER SERVING	KCAL	FATgm	CHOLmg	SODmg
	45	0.4	0	2

Pineapple-Stuffed Pears

Serve this dessert at your next dinner party and you'll be the talk of the town!

MAKES 6 SERVINGS

1 cup sweet red wine
⅓ cup sugar
⅛ teaspoon ground cloves
3 pears, cut in half and cored
½ cup unsweetened pineapple chunks

½ cup unsweetened pineapple juice
6 tablespoons frozen reduced-calorie whipped topping, thawed

In a 5-quart Dutch oven over high heat, bring the wine, sugar and cloves to a boil. Arrange the pears, flat side down, in the Dutch oven and cook, covered, for 20 minutes, or until the liquid is reduced to ½ cup; remove from the heat and reserve the liquid. Remove the pears and let cool to the touch.

Using a spoon, carefully scoop out the center of each pear half, leaving a ½-inch shell. Chop the pear pulp and place in a small bowl. Add the pineapple chunks and juice; mix well. Place the pear shells on a plate and spoon equal amounts of the mixture into each one. Pour the reserved cooking liquid over the pears, then top each with 1 tablespoon of whipped topping.

PER SERVING	KCAL	FATgm	CHOLmg	SODmg
	130	0.4	0	26

Pineapple Delight

MAKES 6 SERVINGS

14 graham crackers
4 ounces reduced-calorie
  soft-style cream cheese
2 cups pineapple sherbet

½ cup canned unsweetened
  crushed pineapple,
  drained

Place the graham crackers in a food processor and process to resemble bread crumbs; reserve ¼ cup. Put the remaining graham cracker crumbs in a medium bowl and add the cream cheese; mix well. Transfer to a 9-inch pie plate and press evenly with your fingertips to cover the entire plate.

Mix together the sherbet and pineapple. Pour into the pie plate and spread evenly. Sprinkle with the reserved graham cracker crumbs. Cover with plastic wrap and freeze.

PER SERVING	KCAL	FATgm	CHOLmg	SODmg
	182	3.8	5	134

Fruit Chutney

MAKES 2½ CUPS

1 cup raisins
1½ cups water
1 medium apple, peeled and
    chopped
1 medium pear, peeled and
    chopped
½ cup unsweetened orange
    juice

2 tablespoons chopped
    orange peel
2 tablespoons lemon juice
1 tablespoon grated fresh
    ginger
1 teaspoon liquid sweetener

Soak the raisins in ½ cup of the water for 1 hour. In a medium skillet over high heat, bring the remaining water to a boil. Reduce the heat to medium. Add the soaked raisins, the soaking water and all the remaining ingredients; cook for 15 minutes, stirring often. Remove from the heat and transfer to a bowl; let cool to the touch. Place half of the mixture in a blender and process until smooth. Return to the bowl and mix well.

PER TABLESPOON	KCAL	FATgm	CHOLmg	SODmg
	16	0	0	1

Quick-and-Easy Pudding

The pineapple and whipped topping give this dish a different twist—with a fraction of the fat and calories in traditional recipes.

MAKES 8 SERVINGS

1 small box instant sugar-free banana pudding mix
2 packets sugar substitute
1½ cups evaporated skim milk
⅛ teaspoon imitation butter flavoring
30 vanilla wafer cookies

1 banana, peeled and thinly sliced
1 cup reduced-calorie whipped topping, thawed
1 cup unsweetened pineapple chunks, drained

In a medium bowl, combine the first 4 ingredients. Beat with an electric mixer on medium speed for 5 minutes, or until the pudding starts to thicken. In a round glass bowl, arrange the vanilla wafers in a single layer. Spoon in *half* of the pudding, then layer with *half* of the bananas, *half* of the pineapple and *half* of the whipped topping. Repeat this process with the remaining ingredients, ending with the whipped topping. Refrigerate for 30 minutes before serving.

PER SERVING	KCAL	FATgm	CHOLmg	SODmg
	135	2.4	11	117

Tyler's Rice Pudding

MAKES 6 SERVINGS

2 cups cooked rice
2 cups evaporated skim
    milk
1 egg
¼ cup light brown sugar
½ teaspoon vanilla extract

¼ teaspoon imitation butter
    flavoring
⅛ teaspoon ground nutmeg
⅛ teaspoon ground allspice
½ cup raisins

Place a 5-quart Dutch oven over high heat. Add the rice and milk; cook and stir for 10 minutes. Add all the remaining ingredients *except* the raisins. Cook and stir 5 minutes longer. Remove from the heat and let cool to the touch, then transfer to a blender. Press the pulse button a few times to break up the rice, but do not puree. Return to the pot and place over medium heat. Add the raisins and cook for another 5 minutes. Spoon into individual serving dishes and serve warm.

PER SERVING	KCAL	FATgm	CHOLmg	SODmg
	176	1.1	49	113

Punch Bowl Cake

We'll let you judge how this delicious dish got its name!

MAKES 10 SERVINGS

1 pound frozen
  unsweetened
  strawberries
¼ teaspoon liquid
  sweetener
One box instant sugar-free
  pistachio pudding mix
2 cups evaporated skim
  milk

2 bananas, peeled and
  thinly sliced
One 11-ounce angel food
  cake, cut into bite-size
  pieces
6 ounces light whipped
  topping

In a small saucepan over medium heat, add the strawberries and sweetener. Cook and stir 5 minutes; set aside. In a medium bowl combine the pudding mix and milk, beat for 5 minutes or until pudding starts to thicken and set aside. In a glass bowl, add half the crumbled cake, half the pudding, half the bananas, half the whipped topping and half the strawberries. Repeat the process with the remaining ingredients, ending with the whipped topping.

PER SERVING	KCAL	FATgm	CHOLmg	SODmg
	212	1	5	175

Brook's Cherry Cobbler

My *great-granddaughter Brook tried this dish just as it was coming out of the oven. She liked it so much, she asked me if she could take it home for dessert!*

MAKES 4 SERVINGS

3 cinnamon-raisin English muffins
1 cup evaporated skim milk

One 16-ounce can light cherry pie filling
2 packets sugar substitute

Preheat the oven to 375°F.

In a food processor, process the muffins until coarsely chopped; transfer to a bowl. Add *half* of the milk and set aside. In a small bowl, combine *half* of the pie filling with the sugar substitute and remaining milk; stir well. Spray the inside of a 9-inch-square baking dish with nonstick vegetable cooking spray. Spoon in *half* of the muffin mixture, then add the pie filling. Top with the remaining muffin mixture and bake for 30 minutes, or until the top is crispy.

PER SERVING	KCAL	FATgm	CHOLmg	SODmg
	269	1.1	3	579

No-Fuss Peach Cobbler

This is a great dessert for those restricted from eating sugar—
and the taste is fantastic!

One 8-ounce box biscuit
   mix
¾ cup unsweetened apple
   juice
One 16-ounce can sliced
   peaches packed in juice
   (do not drain)

¼ teaspoon liquid sugar
   substitute
¼ teaspoon ground apple-
   pie spice

Preheat the oven to 350°F.

In a medium bowl, combine the biscuit mix and apple juice.
Pour *half* of the batter into a 9-inch-square baking dish that has
been sprayed with nonstick vegetable cooking spray; reserve the
remaining batter.

In a small saucepan over high heat, mix the juice from the
peaches, the liquid sugar substitute and apple-pie spice and bring
to a boil. Cook for 2 minutes, or until the liquid is reduced to about
½ cup.

Arrange the peach slices over the batter; pour the liquid over
the peaches, then top with the remaining batter. Bake for 30
minutes, or until brown.

PER SERVING	KCAL	FATgm	CHOLmg	SODmg
	31	0.4	0	36

Double Chocolate Brownies

*H*ere's to all you chocolate lovers!

Makes 12 servings

1 cup cake flour
2 tablespoons unsweetened cocoa
½ teaspoon baking powder
¼ teaspoon salt
1 cup skim milk
3 tablespoons reduced-calorie margarine
One-half 8-ounce carton frozen egg substitute, thawed

½ teaspoon imitation butter flavoring
½ teaspoon imitation chocolate flavoring
2 tablespoons liquid sugar substitute
1 teaspoon cornstarch
½ cup finely chopped pecans

Preheat the oven to 375°F.

In a small bowl, sift together the flour, cocoa, baking powder and salt. In a medium bowl, combine *half* of the milk, the margarine, egg substitute and both flavorings. Mix well and slowly add to the flour mixture, stirring well.

Spray the inside of a 9-inch-square baking dish with nonstick vegetable cooking spray. Spoon the batter into the dish and bake for 15 minutes.

Meanwhile, in a small saucepan over high heat, bring the remaining milk, sugar substitute and cornstarch to a boil. Cook and stir for 3 minutes. Remove from the heat and pour the sauce over the brownies. Top with the pecans.

PER SERVING	KCAL	FATgm	CHOLmg	SODmg
	96	4.6	1	116

Dump Cake

MAKES 10 SERVINGS

*1 box 94% fat-free white
    cake mix
3 egg whites
1½ cups water
One 21-ounce can light
    strawberry pie filling*

*One 16-ounce can crushed
    pineapple packed in
    juice, drained*

Preheat the oven to 350°F.

In a medium bowl, combine the cake mix, egg whites and water. Beat with an electric mixer on low speed for 30 seconds. Spray the inside of a 9-by-11-inch baking dish with nonstick vegetable cooking spray. Pour in *half* of the cake batter; "dump" in the pie filling and pineapple. Spoon the remaining cake batter on top and bake for 35 minutes, or until the cake tests done.

PER SERVING	KCAL	FATgm	CHOLmg	SODmg
	45	1.1	6	45

Cheesecake

MAKES 12 SERVINGS

FOR THE CRUST
⅔ cup graham cracker
   crumbs
2½ teaspoons reduced-
   calorie margarine,
   melted
¼ teaspoon unflavored
   gelatin

FOR THE FILLING
1 envelope unflavored
   gelatin
1 cup cold water

One 8-ounce package
   reduced-calorie soft-
   style cream cheese
1 cup evaporated skim milk
¼ cup sugar
1 tablespoon lemon juice
¼ teaspoon grated lemon
   rind
One 4-ounce package
   instant vanilla pudding
   mix

Place the cracker crumbs, margarine and gelatin in a small bowl
and mix well. Spray the inside of a 9-inch pie plate with nonstick
vegetable cooking spray; add the graham cracker mixture and
press evenly in the pie plate. Bake for 5 minutes, or until lightly
browned. Remove from the oven and let cool on wire rack.

In a small saucepan, sprinkle the gelatin over the water and let
stand for 5 minutes. Place the saucepan over low heat; cook and
stir for 3 minutes, or until the gelatin is dissolved. Combine the
cream cheese, milk, sugar, lemon juice and lemon rind in a medium bowl and beat with a wire whisk. Add the dissolved gelatin
and pudding mix; whisk until smooth. Pour into the pie crust and
refrigerate for 4 hours before serving.

PER SERVING	KCAL	FATgm	CHOLmg	SODmg
	92	1.7	1	134

Glazed Cake Doughnuts

This is a great after-school snack for hungry kids. The margarine makes these doughnuts crisp—and great-tasting.

MAKES 12 DOUGHNUTS

½ cup sugar
¼ cup evaporated skim
   milk
¼ cup reduced-calorie
   margarine
1 egg
2 egg whites
2½ cups flour
2 teaspoons baking powder
1 teaspoon vanilla extract

½ teaspoon ground apple-
   pie spice
¼ teaspoon salt

FOR THE GLAZE

¼ cup water
⅛ teaspoon imitation butter
   flavoring
⅛ teaspoon ground apple-
   pie spice

Preheat the oven to 350°F.

In a medium bowl, combine the sugar, milk, margarine, egg and egg whites. Beat with an electric mixer on low speed for 2 minutes, or until creamy. Add the remaining ingredients and continue beating until the flour is well incorporated. Increase the mixer speed to medium and beat 2 minutes longer. Cover the bowl and chill the dough for 30 minutes.

Place the dough on a clean, floured surface and roll out to a ½-inch thickness. Cut out doughnuts with a doughnut cutter. (You can roll out any leftover dough into any shape you like, this is fun

and prevents waste.) Spray the inside of a baking sheet with non-stick vegetable cooking spray. Arrange the doughnuts on the sheet and bake for 20 minutes.

To Prepare the Glaze: Combine all ingredients in a medium bowl and mix well. Dip each doughnut in the glaze while it is still hot. Place the doughnuts back on the baking sheet to cool.

PER SERVING	KCAL	FATgm	CHOLmg	SODmg
	132	2.6	23	107

Banana Spice Cake

Make this cake, and it will be gone before you have the time to pass the word around that it is ready!

MAKES 12 SERVINGS

2 egg whites
1 egg
1 cup light brown sugar
1 cup dark brown sugar
¼ cup vegetable shortening
½ teaspoon vanilla extract
2 cups cake flour
1 tablespoon baking powder
½ teaspoon salt

½ teaspoon ground
    cinnamon
½ teaspoon ground allspice
¼ teaspoon ground nutmeg
2 large bananas, peeled and
    mashed
½ cup evaporated skim
    milk

Preheat the oven to 350°F.

In a medium bowl, combine the first 6 ingredients. Beat with an electric mixer on medium speed for 1 minute, or until mixed well. In a separate bowl, sift together the flour, baking powder, salt, cinnamon, allspice and nutmeg. Gradually add to the egg mixture along with the bananas and milk. Pour the batter into an 8-inch-round cake pan that has been sprayed with nonstick vegetable cooking spray. Bake for 30 minutes, or until the cake tests done.

PER SERVING	KCAL	FATgm	CHOLmg	SODmg
	252	5	23	204

Index

Alligator stir-fry, 86
Almonds, tilapia with, 73
Amberjack, 74–77
  baked, 75
  grilled, with spinach sauce, 76–77
  poached, with raspberry vinegar
    sauce, 74
Ambrosia, 302
Angelhair pasta:
  chicken-tomato soup with, 6
  with turkey sausage, tomato and
    basil, 256
Apple(s):
  and pork medallions, 182
  and prune tenderloin, 180–181
Apricots, chicken with, 110

Bacon, Canadian:
  breakfast casserole, 227
  rotini with, 249
  split peas with, 191
Bacon, turkey:
  and cheese, baked turnips with, 199
  fresh snap beans with, 189
Banana:
  crunch, 301
  spice cake, 316
Basil:
  and carrots, rotini with, 248
  and sun-dried tomatoes, linguine
    with, 253
  turkey sausage and tomato,
    angelhair pasta with, 256
Bean(s):
  fresh snap, with turkey bacon, 189
  guacamole sauce, 285

refried, 190
salad, three-, 20
Beef, 149–163
  curry, 157
  enchiladas, 163
  fajitas, 158–159
  meat-stuffed bell peppers, 222–223
  Moss Street sirloin, 149
  one-skillet sirloin and vegetables,
    154
  orzo soup, spicy, 7
  -rice casserole, quick-and-easy,
    242
  Sam's cubed, in brown gravy, 156
  smothered steak, 150
  steak and tomatoes, 151
  stew, Prudhomme-style, 243
  stir-fried, 155
  stuffed rolled steak, 152–153
  tamales, 160–161
  and vegetables, 162
Bell pepper(s):
  baked stuffed turnips, 198
  meat-stuffed, 222–223
  rice-stuffed, 218–219
  roasted, 220
  roasted, and crabmeat, corn with,
    221
  smothered okra, 193
  smothered steak, 150
  stuffed Cornish hens, 116
  three-pepper chicken enchiladas,
    106–107
  two-pepper pork chops, 165
Biscuits, granola, 298
Bisque, crabmeat, 10

Blake's chocolate bread, 295–296
Blue cheese chicken, 115
Bow-tie pasta and tuna, 250
Bread, 293–298
    Blake's chocolate, 295–296
    granola biscuits, 298
    plain muffins, 297
    three-pepper, 293–294
Breakfast casserole, 227
Brett's chicken spaghetti, 258
Broccoli:
    au gratin, 211
    and cabbage slaw, 27
    herbed, 210
Brook's cherry cobbler, 309
Brown gravy:
    rabbit in, 186
    Sam's cubed beef in, 156
Brownies, double chocolate, 311
Brown rice pilaf, grilled shrimp with, 54
Brussels sprouts with Dijon mustard, 200
Burritos, turkey, 134–135
Buttermilk:
    chicken, 97
    salad dressing, 30

Cabbage, 25–28
    and broccoli slaw, 27
    "crabby" coleslaw, 26
    and leek soup, 12
    rolls with mushroom sauce, 202–203
    slaw, 25
    sweet-and-sour, 201
    sweet potato slaw with raisin dressing, 28
    and turkey casserole, 236–237
Cajun gazpacho, 15
Cake, 312–316
    banana spice, 316
    cheesecake, 313
    doughnuts, glazed, 314–315
    dump, 312
    punch bowl, 308
Canadian bacon:
    breakfast casserole, 227
    rotini with, 249
    split peas with, 191

Carrot(s):
    and basil, rotini with, 248
    marinated, 206
    and prunes, 208
    and raisin salad, 21
    spicy glazed, 207
Casserole, 225–242
    breakfast, 227
    cauliflower and leek, 228
    cheesy lemon-chicken and rice, 232
    C.J.'s enchilada, 240–241
    oyster, 229
    quick-and-easy beef-rice, 242
    spicy turkey and pasta, 233
    tuna, with penne pasta, 230–231
    turkey and cabbage, 236–237
    turkey and rice, 234–235
    turkey-mirliton, 238–239
Catfish, 82–85
    crispy spicy, 82
    Florentine, 84–85
    oven-fried, 83
Cauliflower:
    creamy, 212
    and leek casserole, 228
    soup, 13
Champagne sauce, orange roughy with, 72
Cheese:
    au gratin potatoes, 194
    and bacon, baked turnips with, 199
    breakfast casserole, 227
    broccoli au gratin, 211
    lemon-chicken and rice casserole, 232
    and macaroni, oven-baked, 259
    sauce, 286
    Southern fettuccine alfredo, 251
    -tomato fettuccine, 252
    topping, for chimi-chimi chicken, 100–101
    see also specific cheeses
Cheesecake, 313
Cheesy lemon-chicken and rice casserole, 232
Cherry cobbler, Brook's, 309
Chicken, 3–6, 87–118
    with apricots, 110
    baked, with fruit chutney, 114

blue cheese, 115
buttermilk, 97
cacciatore, 98
chili, 99
chimi-chimi, 100–101
crispy oven-fried, 90
curried, 108–109
divine, 96
and dumplings, 112–113
enchiladas, 104–105
enchiladas, three-pepper, 106–107
honey roasted, 92–93
lasagna, 262–263
-lemon and rice casserole, cheesy, 232
lemon baked, 91
-lemon soup, Dessire's, 4
no-fuss baked, 89
in red wine sauce, 95
south of the border, 102–103
spaghetti, Brett's, 258
stock, 3
-stuffed mushrooms, 214–215
sweet-and-sour, 94
with sweet potatoes, 111
-tomato soup with pasta, 6
-vegetable soup, 5
see also Cornish hen(s)
Chili:
chicken, 99
Texas, 133
-tomato sauce, 100–101
Chili pepper(s):
bread, three-, 293–294
-lime sauce, tangy sautéed shrimp with, 42
shrimp and jalapeño dip, 280
Chimi-chimi chicken, 100–101
Chocolate:
bread, Blake's, 295–296
brownies, double, 311
Chowder, shrimp, 9
Chutney, fruit, 305
baked chicken with, 114
C.J.'s enchilada casserole, 240–241
Cobbler:
Brook's cherry, 309
no-fuss peach, 310
Coleslaw, see Slaw

Corn:
with crabmeat and roasted peppers, 221
grilled or baked herb, 197
Cornish hen(s), 116–118
old-fashioned pot-roasted, 117
oven-barbecued, 118
stuffed, 116
Corn salsa, 282
grilled salmon with, 70
Crab, crabmeat:
bisque, 10
coleslaw, 26
and roasted peppers, corn with, 221
-stuffed mushrooms, 213
-stuffed party tomatoes, 41
stuffed shrimp, 50
stuffing, rainbow trout with, 64–65
"Crabby" coleslaw, 26
Cranberry vinaigrette, 37
Crawfish sauce, grilled flounder with, 66–67
Cream, creamy:
cauliflower, 212
dill dressing, 31
-lemon sauce, stuffed rabbit legs with, 184–185
sauce, pork chops in, 170–171
sauce, slipper lobsters in, 59
-wine sauce, monkfish medallions with, 80–81
Creole okra, 192
Cucumber:
shrimp-stuffed, baskets, 55
and tomato dressing, 34
and tomato salsa, 281
Curry(ied):
beef, 157
chicken, 108–109
sauce, 287
sauce, pork loin with, 174–175
shrimp, 47
Desserts, 299–316
ambrosia, 302
banana crunch, 301
banana spice cake, 316
Brook's cherry cobbler, 309
cheesecake, 313
double chocolate brownies, 311
dump cake, 312

Desserts (*continued*)
  fruit chutney, 305
  glazed cake doughnuts, 314–315
  no-fuss peach cobbler, 310
  pineapple delight, 304
  pineapple-stuffed pears, 303
  punch bowl cake, 308
  quick-and-easy pudding, 306
  Tyler's rice pudding, 307
Dessire's lemon-chicken soup, 4
Dill dressing, creamy, 31
Dip:
  shrimp and jalapeño, 280
  vegetable, 279
Double chocolate brownies, 311
Doughnuts, glazed cake, 314–315
Dressing, 28–37
  buttermilk salad, 30
  cranberry vinaigrette, 37
  creamy dill, 31
  eggplant rice, 275
  lemon-Parmesan, 32
  raisin, sweet potato slaw with, 28–29
  sour cream, 35
  sour cream, steamed salmon with, 71
  Thousand Island, 33
  tomato and cucumber, 34
  tomato vinaigrette, 36
Drunken sweet potato pone, 195
Dump cake, 312
Dumplings and chicken, 112–113

Eggplant:
  rice dressing, 275
  shrimp-stuffed, 48
  soup, 11
Enchilada(s):
  beef, 163
  casserole, C.J.'s, 240–241
  chicken, 104–105
  shrimp, 44–45
  three-pepper chicken, 106–107
  turkey, 138–139

Fajitas, beef, 158–159
Fettuccine:
  alfredo, Southern, 251
  lemon-Parmesan pasta salad, 265
  tomato-cheese, 252

Fish, 61–86
  amberjack with spinach sauce, grilled, 76–77
  baked amberjack, 75
  catfish Florentine, 84–85
  crispy spicy catfish, 82
  flounder with crawfish sauce, grilled, 66–67
  linguine with tuna, 254–255
  monkfish Florentine, 78–79
  monkfish medallions with wine-cream sauce, 80–81
  orange roughy with Champagne sauce, 72
  oven-fried catfish, 83
  panfried salmon patties, 69
  poached amberjack with raspberry vinegar sauce, 74
  pompano, grilled, 68
  rainbow trout with crab stuffing, 64–65
  salmon with corn salsa, grilled, 70
  steamed salmon with sour cream dressing, 71
  swordfish with tarragon and vermouth, 63
  tilapia with almonds, 73
  tuna and bow-tie pasta, 250
  tuna casserole with penne pasta, 230–231
Flounder, grilled, with crawfish sauce, 66–67
Flour, roux, 289
Fruit chutney, 305
  baked chicken with, 114

Garlic, roasted, and zucchini, 209
Gazpacho, Cajun, 15
Gingersnap gravy, pork chops with, 167
Goulash, Mexican, 140–141
Granola biscuits, 298
Gravy:
  brown, rabbit in, 186
  brown, Sam's cubed beef in, 156
  gingersnap, pork chops with, 167
  mushroom, turkey meatballs with, 126–127
Grits and turkey grand coteau, 123
Guacamole sauce, 285

Hen(s), Cornish, 116–118
old-fashioned pot-roasted, 117
oven-barbecued, 118
stuffed, 116
Herb corn, grilled or baked, 197
Herbed broccoli, 210
Honey:
-mustard turkey, 121
roasted chicken, 92–93
Horseradish shrimp, lemon-pepper, 43
Hot pork tenderloin, 166

Italian turkey with mushrooms, 130–131

Jalapeño and shrimp dip, 280

Lasagna:
chicken, 262–263
vegetable, 264
Leek:
and cabbage soup, 12
and cauliflower casserole, 228
Lemon:
baked chicken, 91
-chicken and rice casserole, cheesy, 232
-chicken soup, Dessire's, 4
-cream sauce, stuffed rabbit legs with, 184–185
guacamole sauce, 285
-Parmesan dressing, 32
-Parmesan pasta salad, 265
-pepper horseradish shrimp, 43
shrimp, sautéed, 52
Lentil soup, Tex-Mex, 14
Lime-pepper sauce, tangy sautéed shrimp with, 42
Linguine:
with sun-dried tomatoes and basil, 253
with tuna, 254–255
Lobsters, slipper, in cream sauce, 59

Macaroni and cheese, oven-baked, 259
Meat:
pan-sautéed veal, 164
pie, turkey and tortilla, 143

-stuffed bell peppers, 222–223
see also Beef; Pork; Pork chops
Meatball(s), turkey:
with mushroom gravy, 126–127
and spaghetti, 128
stew, 244
Meat loaf:
sauce, 288
turkey, 132
Mexican fare:
goulash, 140–141
turkey pie, 136–137
Mirliton:
medley, 205
-turkey casserole, 238–239
turkey-stuffed, 124–125
Monkfish:
Florentine, 78–79
medallions with wine-cream sauce, 80–81
Moss Street sirloin, 149
Muffins, plain, 297
Mushroom(s), 213–217
chicken-stuffed, 214–215
crab-stuffed, 213
gravy, turkey meatballs with, 126–127
Italian turkey with, 130–131
sauce, cabbage rolls with, 202–203
sausage-stuffed, 216–217
Mustard:
Dijon, Brussels sprouts with, 200
-honey turkey, 121
sauce, 284

No-fuss baked chicken, 89
No-fuss peach cobbler, 310

Okra:
creole, 192
smothered, 193
Old-fashioned pot-roasted hen, 117
One-skillet sirloin and vegetables, 154
Onions:
baked stuffed turnips, 198
smothered okra, 193
smothered steak, 150
stuffed Cornish hens, 116
Orange roughy with Champagne sauce, 72

Orzo beef soup, spicy, 7
Oyster(s):
  baked, with shrimp, 56–57
  casserole, 229
  spicy Louisiana, 58

Pancakes, potato, 196
Paprika pork chops, 176
Parmesan-lemon dressing, 32
  pasta salad with, 265
Pasta, 245–265
  angelhair, with turkey sausage,
    tomato and basil, 256
  bow-tie, and tuna, 250
  Brett's chicken spaghetti, 258
  chicken lasagna, 262–263
  chicken-tomato soup with, 6
  linguine with sun-dried tomatoes
    and basil, 253
  linguine with tuna, 254–255
  Mexican goulash, 140–141
  oven-baked macaroni and cheese,
    259
  penne, tuna casserole with, 230–
    231
  rotini with Canadian bacon, 249
  rotini with carrots and basil, 248
  salad, lemon-Parmesan, 265
  Southern fettuccine alfredo, 251
  spicy beef orzo soup, 7
  spicy turkey sausage rotini, 247
  stuffed jumbo shells with tomato
    sauce, 260–261
  tomato-cheese fettuccine, 252
  and turkey casserole, spicy, 233
  turkey meatballs and spaghetti,
    128
  vermicelli with fresh tomato sauce,
    257
Peach cobbler, no-fuss, 310
Pea(s):
  split, with Canadian bacon, 191
  sweet, salad, 19
Pears, pineapple-stuffed, 303
Penne pasta, tuna casserole with,
    230–231
Pepper(s), bell:
  baked stuffed turnips, 198
  -lime sauce, tangy sautéed shrimp
    with, 42

meat-stuffed, 222–223
rice-stuffed, 218–219
roasted, 220
roasted, and crabmeat, corn with,
    221
smothered okra, 193
smothered steak, 150
stuffed Cornish hens, 116
three-pepper chicken enchiladas,
    106–107
two-pepper pork chops, 165
Pepper(s), chili:
  -lime sauce, tangy sautéed shrimp
    with, 42
  shrimp and jalapeño dip, 280
  three-pepper bread, 293–294
Pepper-lemon horseradish shrimp, 43
Pie:
  Mexican turkey, 136–137
  turkey and tortilla meat, 143
Pilaf, brown rice, grilled shrimp with,
    54
Pineapple:
  delight, 304
  dump cake, 312
  -stuffed pears, 303
Plum sauce, pork medallions with,
    179
Pompano, grilled, 68
Pone, drunken sweet potato, 195
Pork, 165–182
  apple and prune tenderloin, 180–
    181
  breakfast casserole, 227
  loin, stuffed, 172–173
  loin with curry sauce, 174–175
  medallions and apples, 182
  medallions with plum sauce, 179
  rotini with Canadian bacon, 249
  split peas with Canadian bacon,
    191
  stir-fry, 177
  sweet-and-sour, 178
  tenderloin, hot, 166
Pork chops, 167–171
  in cream sauce, 170–171
  with gingersnap gravy, 167
  paprika, 176
  in sherry sauce, 168–169
  two-pepper, 165

Potato(es):
  au gratin, 194
  pancakes, 196
  salad, 24
  see also Sweet potato(es)
Prune(s):
  and apple tenderloin, 180–181
  and carrots, 208
Pudding:
  quick-and-easy, 306
  Tyler's rice, 307
Punch bowl cake, 308

Rabbit, 183–186
  in brown gravy, 186
  legs with lemon-cream sauce,
    stuffed, 184–185
  in red wine sauce, spicy, 183
Rainbow trout with crab stuffing, 64–65
Raisin:
  and carrot salad, 21
  dressing, sweet potato slaw with,
    28–29
Raspberry vinegar sauce, poached
    amberjack with, 74
Red wine sauce:
  chicken in, 95
  spicy rabbit in, 183
Refried beans, 190
Rice, 267–275
  baked Texas, 272–273
  basic white, 269
  -beef casserole, quick-and-easy,
    242
  and cheesy lemon-chicken
    casserole, 232
  eggplant dressing, 275
  pilaf, brown, grilled shrimp with, 54
  pudding, Tyler's, 307
  and shrimp, spicy, 49
  Spanish, 271
  -stuffed bell peppers, 218–219
  taco, 274
  and turkey casserole, 234–235
  vegetarian, 270
Rotini:
  with Canadian bacon, 249
  with carrots and basil, 248
  Mexican goulash, 140–141
  spicy turkey sausage, 247

Roughy, orange, with Champagne
    sauce, 72
Roux flour, 289

Salad, 17–29
  carrot and raisin, 21
  lemon-Parmesan pasta, 265
  potato, 24
  sweet pea, 19
  taco, 22–23
  three-bean, 20
  see also Slaw
Salad dressing, 30–37
  buttermilk, 30
  cranberry vinaigrette, 37
  lemon-Parmesan, 32
  sour cream, 35
  Thousand Island, 33
  tomato and cucumber, 34
  tomato vinaigrette, 36
Salmon, 69–71
  grilled, with corn salsa, 70
  patties, panfried, 69
Salmon *(continued)*
  steamed, with sour cream
    dressing, 71
Salsa, 281–283
  corn, 282
  corn, grilled salmon with, 70
  cucumber and tomato, 281
  taco, 283
  see also Sauce
Sam's cubed beef in brown gravy, 156
Sauce:
  Champagne, orange roughy with,
    72
  cheese, 286
  crawfish, grilled flounder with, 66–
    67
  cream, pork chops in, 170–171
  cream, slipper lobsters in, 59
  curry, 287
  curry, pork loin with, 174–175
  fresh tomato, vermicelli with, 257
  guacamole, 285
  lemon-cream, stuffed rabbit legs
    with, 184–185
  meat loaf, 288
  mushroom, cabbage rolls with,
    202–203

Sauce (*continued*)
  mustard, 284
  pepper-lime, tangy sautéed shrimp
    with, 42
  plum, pork medallions with, 179
  raspberry vinegar, poached
    amberjack with, 74
  red wine, chicken in, 95
  red wine, spicy rabbit in, 183
  roux flour, 289
  sherry, pork chops in, 168–169
  shrimp, piquant, 53
  spinach, grilled amberjack with,
    76–77
  tomato, stuffed jumbo shells with,
    260–261
  tomato-chili, 100–101
  wine-cream, monkfish medallions
    with, 80–81
  see also Dressing; Gravy; Salsa
Sausage, turkey:
  rotini, spicy, 247
  smoked, 144–145
  -stuffed mushrooms, 216–217
  tomato and basil, angelhair pasta
    with, 256
Scallops marinara, 60
Shellfish, 39–60
  baked oysters with shrimp, 56–
    57
  corn with crabmeat and roasted
    peppers, 221
  "crabby" coleslaw, 26
  crabmeat bisque, 10
  crab-stuffed mushrooms, 213
  crab-stuffed party tomatoes, 41
  curried shrimp, 47
  flounder with crawfish sauce,
    grilled, 66–67
  lemon-pepper horseradish shrimp,
    43
  oyster casserole, 229
  rainbow trout with crab stuffing,
    64–65
  sautéed lemon shrimp, 52
  scallops marinara, 60
  shrimp and jalapeño dip, 280
  shrimp chowder, 9
  shrimp enchiladas, 44–45
  shrimp sauce piquant, 53

  shrimp-stuffed cucumber baskets,
    55
  shrimp-stuffed eggplant, 48
  shrimp with brown rice pilaf,
    grilled, 54
  slipper lobsters in cream sauce, 59
  spicy Louisiana oysters, 58
  spicy shrimp and rice, 49
  stuffed shrimp, 50–51
  sweet-and-sour shrimp, 46
  tangy sautéed shrimp with pepper-
    lime sauce, 42
Shells, stuffed jumbo, with tomato
  sauce, 260–261
Sherry sauce, pork chops in, 168–
  169
Shrimp, 42–57
  baked oysters with, 56–57
  chowder, 9
  curried, 47
  enchiladas, 44–45
  grilled, with brown rice pilaf, 54
  and jalapeño dip, 280
  lemon-pepper horseradish, 43
  and rice, spicy, 49
  sauce piquant, 53
  sautéed lemon, 52
  stuffed, 50–51
  -stuffed cucumber baskets, 55
  -stuffed eggplant, 48
  sweet-and-sour, 46
  tangy sautéed, with pepper-lime
    sauce, 42
Sirloin:
  Moss Street, 149
  and vegetables, one-skillet, 154
Slaw, 25–29
  broccoli and cabbage, 27
  cabbage, 25
  "crabby" coleslaw, 26
  sweet potato, with raisin dressing,
    28–29
Slipper lobsters in cream sauce, 59
Snap beans with turkey bacon, fresh,
  189
Soup, 1–15
  cabbage and leek, 12
  Cajun gazpacho, 15
  cauliflower, 13
  chicken stock, 3

chicken-tomato, with pasta, 6
chicken-vegetable, 5
crabmeat bisque, 10
Dessire's lemon-chicken, 4
eggplant, 11
shrimp chowder, 9
simple vegetable, 8
spicy beef orzo, 7
split peas with Canadian bacon, 191
Tex-Mex lentil, 14
Sour cream dressing, 35
steamed salmon with, 71
Southern fettuccine alfredo, 251
South of the border chicken, 102–103
Spaghetti:
 Brett's chicken, 258
 and turkey meatballs, 128
Spanish rice, 271
Spice cake, banana, 316
Spinach:
 catfish Florentine, 84–85
 monkfish Florentine, 78–79
 sauce, grilled amberjack with, 76–77
 stuffed pork loin, 172–173
 stuffed rabbit legs with lemon-cream sauce, 184–185
 tangy, 204
Split peas with Canadian bacon, 191
Steak, 149–154
 Moss Street sirloin, 149
 one-skillet sirloin and vegetables, 154
 smothered, 150
 stuffed rolled, 152–153
 and tomatoes, 151
 see also Beef
Stew:
 beef, Prudhomme-style, 243
 turkey meatball, 244
Stock, chicken, 3
Stuffing, crab, rainbow trout with, 64–65
Sun-dried tomatoes and basil, linguine with, 253
Sweet-and-sour:
 cabbage, 201
 chicken, 94
 pork, 178
 shrimp, 46

Sweet pea salad, 19
Sweet potato(es):
 chicken with, 111
 pone, drunken, 195
 slaw with raisin dressing, 28–29
Swordfish with tarragon and vermouth, 63

Taco:
 rice, 274
 salad, 22–23
 salsa, 283
Tamales, beef, 160–161
Tarragon and vermouth, swordfish with, 63
Texas chili, 133
Tex-Mex lentil soup, 14
Thousand Island dressing, 33
Three-bean salad, 20
Three-pepper:
 bread, 293–294
 chicken enchiladas, 106–107
Tilapia with almonds, 73
Tomato(es):
 baked stuffed turnips, 198
 Cajun gazpacho, 15
 -cheese fettuccine, 252
 chicken cacciatore, 98
 -chicken soup with pasta, 6
 -chili sauce, 100–101
 crab-stuffed party, 41
 and cucumber dressing, 34
 and cucumber salsa, 281
 sauce, fresh, vermicelli with, 257
 sauce, stuffed jumbo shells with, 260-261
 scallops marinara, 60
 smothered okra, 193
 Spanish rice, 271
 and steak, 151
 sun-dried, and basil, linguine with, 253
 turkey sausage and basil, angelhair pasta with, 256
 vinaigrette, 36
Tortilla(s):
 beef fajitas, 158–159
 south of the border chicken, 102–103
 turkey burritos, 134–135

325

Tortilla(s) (*continued*)
  and turkey meat pie, 143
  see also Enchiladas
Trout, rainbow, with crab stuffing,
  64–65
Tuna:
  and bow-tie pasta, 250
  casserole with penne pasta, 230–
   231
  linguine with, 254–255
Turkey, 119–146, 234–239
  bacon, fresh snap beans with,
   189
  baked turnips with bacon and
   cheese, 199
  breasts, baked, 119
  burritos, 134–135
  and cabbage casserole, 236–
   237
  Cornish hens, stuffed, 116
  enchiladas, 138–139
  fiesta, 142
  and grits grand coteau, 123
  honey-mustard, 121
  jumbo shells with tomato sauce,
   stuffed, 260–261
  kabobs, 129
  Lafayette, 122
  meat loaf, 132
  Mexican goulash, 140–141
  -mirliton casserole, 238–239
  with mushrooms, Italian, 130–
   131
  and pasta casserole, spicy, 233
  pie, Mexican, 136–137
  and rice casserole, 234–235
  -stuffed mirliton, 124–125
  Texas chili, 133
  and tortilla meat pie, 143
  -vegetable stir-fry, 120
Turkey meatball(s):
  with mushroom gravy, 126–127
  and spaghetti, 128
  stew, 244

Turkey sausage:
  rotini, spicy, 247
  smoked, 144–145
  -stuffed mushrooms, 216–217
  tomato and basil, angelhair pasta
   with, 256
Turnips:
  with bacon and cheese, baked, 199
  baked stuffed, 198
Two-pepper pork chops, 165
Tyler's rice pudding, 307

Veal, pan-sautéed, 164
Vegetable(s), 187–224
  and beef, 162
  -chicken soup, 5
  dip, 279
  lasagna, 264
  and sirloin, one-skillet, 154
  soup, simple, 8
  turkey fiesta, 142
  -turkey stir-fry, 120
  see also specific vegetables
Vegetarian rice, 270
Vermicelli with fresh tomato sauce,
  257
Vermouth and tarragon, swordfish
  with, 63
Vinaigrette:
  cranberry, 37
  tomato, 36
Vinegar:
  raspberry sauce, poached
   amberjack with, 74
  tangy spinach, 204

White rice, basic, 269
Wine-cream sauce, monkfish
  medallions with, 80–81
Wine sauce, red:
  chicken in, 95
  spicy rabbit in, 183

Zucchini and roasted garlic, 209